D1053724

THE JOY OF MEDITATION

By

JACK and CORNELIA ADDINGTON

DeVORSS & CO., *Publishers*
P.O. Box 550
Marina del Rey, CA 90294

Library of Congress Catalog Number: 78-75078

ISBN: 0-87516-292-4

Fifth Printing, 1988

Cover design by Della Lawrence

Printed in the United States of America

This book is dedicated to all who have found meditation to be the way to Reality.

CONTENTS

Meditation is simply prayer without words, prayer of the soul and mind and heart. In its best form, it is like talking to God with the tongue of the spirit and hearing Him answer with the ears of the soul. It is spiritual training. It is filled with consolations unknown to those who never practice it.

Meditation at its poorest is the highest form of prayer, but at its best it is a foretaste of Heaven's joy.

—Bishop F. C. Kelley

INTRODUCTION

It was meditation that caused me to leave my successful law practice just when I was getting it firmly established. The legal profession was a goal I had worked long and hard to achieve. The experience of meditation opened up a new world to me. Through meditation I gained inner strength and came to know my true self. Meditation was my escape into Reality. I came to see that my thinking had been based on popular premises that were not necessarily true. This involved religion, health, human relationships and every part of life. A whole new world of Truth began to open up for me. I could not wait to share it with others. After I learned to meditate, I was no longer content with the business world. My drive was turned in the direction of a complete dedication to sharing the spiritual life with others.

As I learned more and more about meditation, I discovered that one did not have to be a hermit, a monk, or live by himself like Thoreau to enjoy meditation. I found the time to meditate in an otherwise busy life. There is a meditative approach that can be introduced into life in many ways.

I think the thing that discourages most people of the Western world is that they think they have to spend hours at a time in meditation. The meditative life can be melded into any life. I became a metaphysical teacher, but one need not leave his chosen career to take up meditation. In this book I hope to show the reader how it can become a part of anyone's life.

It is easier to talk about a journey than to actually travel it; yet the real joy is in the journey. In this book we are interested in the experience of meditation; we want you to experience the various ways of meditation rather than just discuss it.

When our daughter was in college, she took a regular Physical Education Course wherein she was allowed an elective. She chose tennis. For three months she had instruction in tennis. Following that, she had private lessons with a tennis pro. One day I challenged her to a game. To my surprise, she said that she would not know how to go about playing a game. She had studied a lot about tennis but she did not know how to play the game.

There are many books about meditation. In this book we will start right in practicing meditation. We want you to experience the joy of meditation, basking in the Spirit as you would bask in the sun.

J.E.A.

Chapter I

PREPARING THE WAY
FOR MEDITATION

Meditation is communing with the Source of all Life, the well-spring of joy. What is joy? It is the emotion of realized good and the expectation of good. Joy is as natural as breathing. It has been built into us. The negative emotions—hate, fear, anger, sorrow and sadness are the by-products of man's human judgments. They are self-induced, but joy is a gift of God. As we commune with the Source we feel joy, that great surge of emotion that tells us we are one with all good. God is joy. Joy is one of the attributes of the Infinite.

Meditation is the only way you can escape from the mortal dream of surface appearance into the joyous Reality of Life. Like a mirage in the desert, the outer world is the dream. It has no more lasting reality than a television movie. Do not feel guilty to step out of this fast-moving world of the senses and, through meditation, enter Reality. The world will wait for you and you will be better able to cope with it when you return. The time you spend in meditation is the most valuable time you will ever spend. It is never wasted. Learn to meditate through practicing meditation. I invite you now to go with me on a wonderful journey of Self-discovery, uncovering the spiritual Self within you.

Leave Your Old Judgments Behind

As you enter into the meditative life you are embarking on a most rewarding adventure. You must begin with a completely open mind. There is nothing quite so exciting. No experience will ever mean more to you. Everything you once thought important will seem empty by comparison. On the other hand, meditation will so enrich your life that everything you do will become more meaningful. Ultimately, you will find that the only lasting joy is to be found in communion with Reality which you experience through meditation. Once you have experienced this you will never again be satisfied to live only for the limited satisfactions of the outer world

Meditation is a Spiritual Experience

There are those who say that meditation is not necessarily a religious experience and can be practiced by anyone simply by repeating over and over a particular word, or combination of words. The kind of meditation I am talking about *is* a spiritual experience. I am not referring to theological dogma but a fact of life. Spirit is. The joy of meditation can be experienced by anyone who is open and receptive to receive from the Spirit within. Spirit, like the wind cannot be seen but we see the evidence of it. *There is a spirit in man: and the inspiration of the Almighty giveth them understanding.*[1] *God is a spirit and they that worship him must worship him in spirit and in truth.*[2]

Getting the Little Self out of the Way

Ask yourself, "Why do I resist meditation?"

Is it because you think you would be bored just sitting and doing nothing? Do you feel guilty to take time out from your busy day? Do you think that action is the answer to your problems? Do you think that inaction is just a waste of time? That just sitting in meditation would be running away from your problems? Do you believe that there is something sacrilegious about making direct contact with God? Are you afraid to look within for fear of what you may find there? Have you become so accustomed to stress that you are afraid of the peace you may find within? Are you discouraged because you tried it once and found it didn't work? Are you afraid of what your friends will say if they hear you have taken up meditation?

[1]Job 32:8
[2]John 4:24

You must recognize all of these questions in your own mind before you will be free to experience meditation. May I help you? Many people resist meditation as one resists the unknown. Most of our resistance comes from prejudice, an opinion or feeling that is based upon judgments of the past. The word prejudice means pre-judgment and many people have pre-judgments about meditation.

For instance, there are those who immediately associate meditation with the Far East, particularly India. When you think of the word *meditation*, do you mentally see a swami, with his head wrapped in a turban, sitting in the lotus position? It is true that swamis meditate, and often reach exalted states of consciousness, but they do not have a corner on meditation.

Another prejudice a person may have is a pre-judgment about anything spiritual. There are those who identify it with a particular theology, a monastic order, or a church. Some people think that anything spiritual has to be pious and involve a sense of long-suffering renunciation. This is all right for those who like it that way.

A Joyous Way of Life

The Master said, *I am come that ye might have life and have it more abundantly.* Think of meditation as a joyous way of life. Recognize that there is a Power greater than you are, right where you are, and that it is a part of your very life and you can use it. You are here to experience the joy of the Spirit within you.

Let Meditation Happen to You

We have all become such busy do-ers that we think we have to make everything happen. Meditation is something that happens to you. It will happen to you if you let it. *Let* is a most important word when it comes to meditation. Complete inaction can be the most active thing you will ever do. An hour in meditation can be more valuable to you than years of hard work. This is what the Master meant by *my yoke is easy, and my burden is light.*

Meditation is drinking deep from the well of the Spirit. The joy of meditation is in the bliss of experiencing union with the One. Meditation is *be still and know that I am God.* In the Silence you can have a two-way meditation. As you meditate on these beautiful words it is as if God says to you:

Be still, my child, and know that I am God within you.

In your mind, you answer back:

I will be still and know that thou art God within me.

Now Let us Practice Meditation Together

Sit quietly in an upright position. Since meditation is an inner [not an outer] thing, posture is not the most important aspect. You may even meditate in bed. The important thing is a relaxed mental attitude. Many people find that this is best achieved in a comfortable, upright position, the hands lying open palms up on the lap, signifying a receptive attitude.

Meditation

Now close your eyes and shut the world of effects out. Jesus called this going into the closet and shutting the door. Let us take for our meditation* the beautiful thought we have mentioned: *Be still and know that I am God.* If your mind wanders, do not be harsh with yourself but patiently bring it back by repeating silently: *Be still and know.*

Be Still and Know That I Am God

*I will be still and know the Spirit of God
within me.*

---

*A word of explanation: We are using words in conveying to you our meditation because that is the only means we have of communicating with you. But, words are not necessarily the way *you* will receive *your* meditation. Meditation is a feeling thing. It comes as a series of impressions, impressions of joy, release, confidence and trust. It may come as a great surge of joy and freedom. It is *your* meditation and the way *you* experience it will be *yours* alone.

*I am still and know that the I Am of God
    lives in me.
I am still. I am centered in perfect peace.
I am still. I know that the I Am of God
    within me lives my life.*

Silence

*The I Am of God within me lights my path,
    directs my way, and accomplishes all that
    is given to me to do.
I know the wonder of God lives through me.
I rejoice in the knowing that of myself I can
    do nothing;
    the Father within me doeth the work.
I let go and let the I Am of God live through
    me in Its perfect way.*

Silence

*I know the Joy of God is my joy; the life of
    God is my life; the Love of God is my love.
All that God is, I am.*

Silence

Chapter II

HOW YOU CAN MEDITATE

Set aside a certain time for meditation each day. Pick the time and then claim it for yourself. Let it be known, "This is my meditation time." Make it known that you are not to be disturbed. If others in the family, or friends, think you are peculiar, let them. This is their problem, not yours. Whatever you do, do not feel ashamed or guilty for taking time out to meditate.

One of the problems people have today is their emphasis on busy-ness. We are all inclined to think that we have to keep doing something every minute, when, in truth, our time in the Silence is the most productive and creative time in the day. *Being* is more important than *doing*. The *doing* will fall into place easily once one has made conscious contact with his Source.

The Mind Can Be Trained

In time, the mind can be trained. If your mind wanders, if you are interrupted, do not feel that all is lost. Patiently bring yourself back into the meditation. You may have to do this many times, but this is all right. Take a patient, lying in the sun, attitude. The telephone may ring. Do not resist it. You can resume your meditation later. Often I have interrupted myself, in meditation, to write down some idea that has come to me. Then I have resumed the meditation. Do not judge yourself. Let your meditation unfold easily.

If you go to sleep in your meditation, do not condemn yourself. Start again; keep with it; have another meditation. If you go to sleep contemplating the Presence, the subconscious mind will continue the meditation.

The Eastern teachers say that the mind is like a monkey, the way it jumps about. If you find yourself making a shopping list during your meditation, if some mundane thought pops into your head, laugh at the monkey and order him out. Patiently bring the mind back into focus. In time, you will find that you can train it to do your bidding. This is why people use a mantra. A mantra is simply a word or words that you choose to use to focus your mind in meditation. Some of the words that can be used are: *God, Christ, peace, love.*

Peace is a wonderful mantra. Do not try to relate this word to things in the outer world. Just live with the word "peace" for as long as you can and let it flower in your mind. You are not trying to be analytical, for meditation is a *feeling thing.* Let *peace* bring you the feeling of peace. *My peace I give unto you,* said the Master, *not as the world gives, give I unto you.* We will be talking more about the mantra in the next chapter.

Relax Into Meditation

In Chapter VI we will be discussing relaxation as a means of entering into meditation. We will show you how to relax your body at will. Relaxation is essential to meditation. It enables one to forget the body.

Meditation Not the Time to Solve Problems

Meditation is not for brooding upon problems, not the time to solve them. It is a time for unifying with the perfect Power within you. When you have done this your problems will find answers easily. So, for the purpose of opening your mind to receive inspiration from within, I suggest that you give your mind directions something like this:

I am now at peace; I am turning away from problems.
I am now opening my mind to receive inspiration from the fount of all inspiration within.

You Cannot Stop Thinking

It is not possible to make your mind a blank. You cannot completely turn your thoughts off. Many people have given up meditation because they found it impossible to make the mind a blank. As you begin to meditate it helps turn the picture off in your mind to imagine a black velvet curtain before the mind's eye. In other words, turn off the television set in your mind! Now, think of some peaceful word or phrase. If your mind wanders, do not blame yourself. Quietly, bring it back to a receptive attitude.

Meditation is Not Necessarily a Supernatural Experience

Do not expect to see lights or experience some supernatural phenomenon. This is not necessary. In time, if you are patient, you will experience all of the joys of meditation. Perhaps as you go along you may have some supernatural experience. You may see lights or smell some exquisite fragrance. Some do. Do not expect this to happen or be disappointed if it is not your experience. However, if you do see lights or have some unusual experience, do not be disappointed if others do not know what you are talking about. It is best not to share these experiences unless you know that you are talking to a kindred soul.

Using a Bible Verse or Other Inspirational Quotation as a Mantra

You may want to start with some favorite Bible verse or other Truth statement and work with it as your mantra. For instance, you might take *Thou wilt keep him in perfect peace whose mind is stayed on thee.* You might take a line from some hymn or poem that inspires you. Anything is useful that helps you open that inner door, any word or thought that helps you center your mind on the Spirit within you. You will know when you have felt the Presence. Meditation is a form of peaceful contemplation. In the end result it is listening to the Spirit within rather than reciting a lot of beautiful words.

Your Meditation Will Become Richer As You Go Along

Your meditation will get richer and deeper as you go along. Release yourself into the meditation. You are not trying to make something happen. You are there to receive from the Spirit within, which is infinite Wisdom and Harmony. *Ask and you shall receive,* in time, a spiritual experience.

Meditation is Highly Personal

No, you do not have to sit in the lotus position; you do not have to sit in the dark; you do not have to see lights and hear strange music—you just have to take the time to be quiet, to still the mind long enough to let the Spirit of Truth within you speak to you in the Silence.

Your meditation will be highly personal to you. Your experience in meditation need not be like mine. Each one will find his own way.

The Rewards Are Great

Do take time to meditate. It is the most wonderful experience you can have. It is mind-expanding; it puts you in tune with the Soul of the Universe, in tune with the Infinite. The fruits of meditation are so lavish and so varied that we cannot possibly convey to you its rich rewards.

But most of all, meditation is its own reward, and should not be entered into for any other reason. As Ernest Holmes once said:

> *The general acceptance of the term meditation is contemplation, or continuous thought. We mean to convey something more. It is truly the recognition of the Father within, the certainty of our Oneness with the Whole, the immediate availability of the Power and Wisdom resulting from this Oneness. Such communion with God brings harmony into our lives and affairs; establishes the law of health and prosperity, and makes us a light to all who cross our pathway.*

It Only Takes a Minute

It is interesting to note that even though Joel Goldsmith sometimes meditated for four or five hours at a time, he said in one of his writings:

It only takes a minute of that silence, of that inner peace, and your meditation is complete, because it really makes no difference whether you see visions, or see colors, or get messages; that is all beside the point, it is not necessary. It sometimes happens, but it is not necessary. The only thing that is necessary is that ability to prepare ourselves for the entrance of God into our conscious thought, be silent for that half a minute, or two minutes, and then be about our business. We have opened the way, and at any given point after that, God will make Itself known to us whenever the necessity arises. We may get our assurance at the moment of meditation, we may not. We may be awakened out of our sleep to receive it, or we may receive it when we are doing our housework, or when we are cooking, or when we are out marketing or shopping, or in our business office. You never know when God will speak to you, or in what way, but of this you may be assured: that living under God's government—God will speak to us.

Listening, Feeling, Perceiving

So far, we have been meditating through the use of the spoken word. Were you here, sitting beside me, we could have just as well had our meditation together in complete silence, for meditation is not necessarily words, it is feeling and deep inner perception. Joel Goldsmith further said:

> *Meditation is much like inviting God to enter us, or to speak to us, or to make itself known to us. It is not an attempt to reach God, since God is Omnipresence. Where God is, I am; where I am, God is, since we are one. So there is no need to reach for God; the purpose is to be still and let the awareness of God permeate us. The activity is always from God to us. We are not seeking to reach God. We start with the realization that where I am, God already is, and therefore we seek a state of stillness in which we may become consciously aware of that Presence. The Presence already is, the Presence always is; in sickness or in health, in lack or in abundance, in sin or in purity, the Presence of God always already is. There is no seeking after it, there is no striving for it, we begin with that realization, God is, God is where I am, I and the Father are one. In that realization you relax and invite the Father to*

reveal Itself: "Speak, Lord, Thy servant heareth." That is really the main function of meditation.

It was Mother Julian of Norwich who said, For every one who says "speak, Lord, thy servant heareth," there are ten who say "hear, Lord, thy servant speaketh."

Meditation

Let us be listeners now and start our meditation together with the words: Speak, Lord, thy servant heareth. Let us sit quietly in the Silence together and listen for the Voice within.

Silence

In the Silence we will hear the Presence
    speak to us:
Be still and know that I am God within you.
And we will answer back: Speak Lord, thy
    servant heareth.
I will be still and hear the voice of God
    within me.

Silence

Chapter III

THE MANTRA IN MEDITATION

Meditation is as natural as breathing. It is as natural as drinking water from a clear stream. Yet it is not something that is done for us automatically. One must consciously still the mind to enter into the Silence. The power of meditation comes from the one Power, the infinite Power. It is God living through us. The Power is always there, ready to express through us. So when we meditate we take conscious action and receive a subconscious response.

"My Yoke is Easy"

No one is going to make us meditate. It is something we must initiate ourselves. If someone has to induce you to meditate, you have missed the point. Meditation is a form of self-discipline. Jesus said, *My yoke is easy.* The yoke comes from the Latin, *jungere,* meaning to join. It means to be joined or intimately associated, to be connected. Shakespeare said, *We will yoke together like a double shadow.* When we meditate we are yoked, or linked with, our divine Source. The word *yoga* is derived from yoke. It is joining with the divine.

Incline Thine Ear

Meditation is not a panacea or cure-all, but meditation opens the way for the divine to come through. *Incline thine ear,* the Bible says. Through meditation we do just that. We listen for the voice of God. Our tendency is to talk too much. Through meditation we become quiet and receptive to the inner Wisdom that flows from the divine Center within each one of us.

All too often when we are doing the talking, or even praying, our talk and our prayers are based upon fear. The Bible says, *God hath not given us the spirit of fear, but of power, and of love, and of a sound mind.*[1] Through the power of love within us, we overcome fear. The divine Center within is a center of Love, and of Power and of perfect balance and justice. This is the kingdom of God within you. We do not see the kingdom of God come into our experience. As Jesus said, *Men cannot say, Look, here it is, or There it is, for the kingdom of God is inside you.*[2]

[1] II Timothy 1:7
[2] Luke 17:20, The Gospels (J.B. Phillips)

When we still the mind and become receptive through meditation, we atune ourselves to the right use of the kingdom of God at the very center of our being. Through meditation, we become whole and complete.

The human tendency is to verbalize all the time, to think about problems, about our environment, about our mental and physical life. That is the reason we seldom hear what is told us from within. But through meditation, our ears are opened to hear. *He that hath an ear, let him hear what the Spirit has to say.*[3] Through meditation we become listeners, ready and able to hear the Truth that is revealed to us from within.

The Mantra in Meditation

Now we will consider the use of the mantra in meditation. A mantra is a word, a phrase, a hymn or a chant used to still the mind, to make it totally receptive to the divine Consciousness. You might like to use *OM* (spelled *OM,* or *AUM*). *Om* as a mantra originated with the Hindus, and is now used by Buddhists and others. It is considered to be the universal vibration. Let the "m" vibrate as a humming sound. This is a wonderful way to bring the focus of the mind back to the center.

[3]Revelation 2:29

The mantra can be used in any of the following: the cleansing meditation, the creative meditation, the contemplative meditation, the healing meditation, the deep meditation, which has been called the mind-expanding meditation. All meditations are transcendental, because in meditation the limitations of the material and mental world are transcended through the inflow from the divine Source within.

A Peace Meditation

All the world is seeking peace, "peace in our time," "world peace," "national peace." But most of all we are seeking individual peace, peace of mind, inner peace, that divine peace *that passeth all understanding*.

To meditate for peace of mind, I use as a mantra the word *peace*. I simply start with the word, *peace*. I think peace, slowly and calmly, over and over—peace . . . peace . . . peace . . .

. . . peace . . .

Allow several minutes of silence between each silent thought of peace. Soon you will be in tune with peace. You will feel the harmony and the tranquility the word carries with it. A feeling of divine Peace will come over you. When someone writes to me who is troubled and up-tight, I meditate on peace. Before long a great feeling of peace fills me.

The Hindu word for peace is *shanti*. You might like to use *shanti* in your meditation. *Shanti* is a beautiful word that carries with it the consciousness of peace. These two words, *peace* and *shanti* carry with them the accumulated peace of the ages.

You might like to use the Hebrew word *shalom*. It also means peace, and isn't it a beautiful word? *Peace—shanti—shalom*—it is impossible to say them without feeling at peace with the oneness of Life.

Another word considered a mantra is *God*. Another is *Christ*. Another is *love*. To say these words over and over is to tune in on the cumulative consciousness of the ages. That little three-letter word, *G–O–D,* is a symbol for all that God is. You will come to see that these words invoke the Power. They are more than a string of letters put together. They carry with them the power with which they have been endowed through years of associating them with the one and only Power.

Any word that is used interchangeably with God, any attribute of God, such as *Peace, Life, Love,* is a good word to use as a mantra. Some people use a Bible verse, such as "Be still and know that I am God." I always add *within you:* Be still and know that I am God within you.

Meditation

Let us join in a meditation for peace:

Peace, be still . . . .
             Peace . . . .
       Peace . . . .
                Peace . . . .
   I am at peace . . . . . .
       I am one with the Peace of God . . . . .
   Peace fills my being . . . . . .

Silence

             Peace be unto you.

Silence

Chapter IV

DIFFERENT WAYS TO MEDITATE

There are no set rules for meditation. Your meditation will be natural to you. You will find what is right for you as you proceed in your search for spiritual awareness and understanding. Meditation is not something that has to be learned by rote. As we learn to meditate, we are opening our minds to an entirely new life, the life of the spirit.

The Cleansing Meditation

The cleansing meditation is based on love. As we go about our daily lives, we are inclined to wrestle with fear, anxiety and jealousy. Fear has so many children! But through the cleansing meditation we open the door to let love in, and love floods out fear and all of the children of fear. In our meditation we do not wrestle with fear or anxiety, but let love cast it out. The Bible says, "Perfect love casts out fear." When we commune with love, fear is dissolved. It simply disappears. I like to think of love as neutralizing fear and all

31

of the children of fear, such as envy, hate, greed, hostility, and more. Meditate on divine love, everywhere present, and your fears will disappear.

Creative Meditation

In creative meditation we let the mind expand and stretch. We open the way for new ideas. Do you need ideas in your business? Do you need new approaches to your family problems? Do you need new understanding for your children and others close to you? You will not uncover the answers by thinking about your problems. But they will come to you when your mind is still. The creativity of life wants to live through you, but it cannot do so while you are setting up the barriers of what you think ought to be done and are stubbornly hanging on to old notions.

Where do ideas come from? Where do inventors get their ideas? How is it possible for a composer to hear in his mind an entire symphony as if it had already been produced? Yet it is entirely new to him. Why are some people more creative than others?

The creative meditation is our contact with divine Intuition. Deep within each one of us is the wisdom of the ages. Hidden within us is an infinite source of creative ideas that can never be exhausted. While we search upon the surface of life for the ideas that we need, frantically turning the pages of books or researching the minds of other people, there exists at the center of our being the very idea that would be perfect for the need. While the conscious mind is stilled, the subconscious mind, acting like a computer, will bring up the information we seek.

Contemplative Meditation

Now, the *contemplative* meditation is the contemplation of God *within*. Emerson said that contemplation is the highest form of prayer. Through contemplation we enter into the kingdom of heaven within us. Through contemplation it is possible to dwell in the kingdom — the kingdom of peace, harmony, wisdom and joy. My own definition of heaven is that state of mind which is founded on peace and love — the love that casts out fear and brings with it joy, happiness and a sense of divine well-being.

It is heaven to feel one with the oneness of Life. Through contemplation we overcome our separate thinking and become consciously one, unified with the oneness of Life.

How do we practice contemplation? Suppose we were to take the word *God* and say it over and over in the mind, and then gradually expand the word into the attributes of God. God is Life, God is Love, God is Peace, God is Power, God is Light, God is Wisdom, God is Joy.

When you have contemplated the attributes of God, identify yourself with each of them. I am Love, I am Life, I am Light, I am Peace, I am Power, I am Wisdom, I am Joy.

Healing Meditation

Any meditation that contemplates the Truth of Being is a healing meditation. Emmet Fox said that the Golden Key is to turn away from the condition and turn the attention to God instead. When we turn away from the outer appearances and think of the divine perfection within, we have, in essence, turned off the condition, for in truth it has only the power we give it. As we meditate on divine perfection we will experience, in exact proportion to our awareness of the Presence, its perfection in our experience. Therefore, it is not necessary to pray for a healing, for as we become in tune with the perfect Life within through meditation, healings will automatically take place.

I have had the experience of spending time in the Silence where I reached a high state of consciousness. Afterward, I have had people call me on the telephone or write to me, telling me that they had thought of me at that time, and had experienced a healing. We are all in one Mind, and the consciousness we experience in meditation is felt by all who turn toward us in thought.

Your meditation period is the most important period in your day. Be eccentric if need be, but take that time. Tell people that this is your time for meditation and that you do not want to be bothered. Go apart and meditate. There is no gift so valuable to yourself, to those in your immediate circle, and to the universal consciousness.

When we raise our consciousness, we raise the consciousness of all mankind.

Deep Meditation

Once we begin to see the part that deep meditation can play in our lives, we begin to feel the power of *Be still and know that I am God.* When we are still, when the mind is quiet, then the inflow of Spirit causes one to experience a new dimension of being. With it comes a realization of the Presence, the spiritual I Am within, the divine Center that is God. Once you begin to still the mind and feel a sense of inner peace, you are ready to listen for the Voice within.

When your mind begins to wander, think again softly to yourself the mantra you have chosen. This is a meditation for the purpose of developing spiritual consciousness. Through deep meditation we achieve an inward feeling of at-one-ment with God. We become in harmony with the universe. After you become adept at meditation you will want to spend as much time as possible in *deep* meditation. But to begin with, if you can spend 15 minutes in the morning and 15 minutes in the evening in meditation, you will begin to open your mind to receive a tremendous inflow of spiritual awareness.

How to Enter Deep Meditation

To enter into deep meditation, we must still the mind to the point where we are open and

receptive to the divine inflow. In deep meditation
we don't need words. It is something that happens
when we have been still long enough to be completely free of outward influences and are no
longer thinking in relative terms. It is when one
becomes so in tune with the Spirit that he is
oblivious to everything but union with the Spirit.
As you practice meditation for longer and longer
periods of time, you will gradually go deeper into
meditation.

Practice using one of the absolute words we
discussed at the beginning of this chapter as a
mantra when the mind begins to wander. The
students of Zen will tell you that your thoughts
must become completely stilled, so that the mind
is virtually a blank. But through experience we
have found that we never come to the place where
the mind is completely still, or a total blank. We
can, though, become still enough to reach that
point of conscious union with the Spirit within,
where we have an overwhelming awareness of the
Presence. More and more we will find that we
enter into a deeper state of consciousness as we
meditate.

Guided Meditation

Throughout this book we will be giving you
guided meditations. Guided meditation is a way
of partaking of another's verbal meditation. If
you are in tune with your spiritual teacher, you
can blend your thought with his in much the
same way that you would sing along with another,

or dance in perfect harmony with another. In a guided meditation, we give you pauses or silences in which you can rest and let your own meditation develop. Take as long as you want to do this. Through guided meditation those who are new to meditation are able to practice meditation.

Now let us have our guided meditation together. Let us take for our inspiration that beautiful verse from the 26th chapter of Isaiah: *Thou wilt keep him in perfect peace, whose mind is stayed on thee, because he trusteth in thee:*

A Guided Meditation

I am the Spirit of God within you.
I give you Peace.

Silence

I am the Christ within you.
I will never leave you.

Silence

I am the Spirit of Truth within you.
I set you free.

Silence

I am divine Love within you that casts out fear.

Silence

Chapter V

STILL OTHER WAYS
TO MEDITATE

Since meditation is such an individual experi-ence, there are as many ways to meditate as there are people. We have a friend who likes to medi-tate in the swimming pool. Great peace comes to her as she floats on the water. An excellent swimmer, she is perfectly confident in the water. It must seem to her that she is *resting on the ever-lasting arms.*

Jesus Set the Highest Standard

I doubt if there is anyone in our present day society who would be willing to go alone to the desert and there fast and meditate for forty days and forty nights, although the desert is a wonder-ful place to meditate. The air is so clear, the stars seem so close you can touch them, and the peace and quiet are ideal for meditation. We often do our writing in the desert where we have a hide-away for that purpose—but forty days and nights alone in meditation we have not tried. Yet, we have no doubt that this would be the way to build a high spiritual consciousness. What? you say. Even the Christ Consciousness? Wasn't that what the man said? *All these things that I do, you can do also, because I go unto my Father.* He communed with the Father Consciousness for forty days and forty nights. He went apart often to meditate and was willing to be alone and hungry. If that's what it took, I say it was well worth it.

In the book of St. John, chapters 15, 16 and 17 are written in a stream of consciousness style. John quoted Jesus throughout, and the words are so beautiful, they are pure music. They could only have come out of meditation. He said that he spoke what he heard. That is why this highly mystical soliloquy is apt to be misunderstood. Jesus himself said that he spoke figurative language; that not all of his hearers were ready for more. It cannot be interpreted in a materialistic way, *but by comparing spiritual things with spiritual; that which is born of the Spirit is spirit.*

The Little Prince Who Became the Buddha

Many years ago in India, legend tells us, a little prince was born whom the sages foretold would become the Buddha, which means "the Enlightened One," or the one who has attained Supreme Wisdom. His name was Siddhartha Gautama. His parents had waited a long time for this child. The King was 50 years old when the baby came, and he was not pleased when the sages prophesied that this was an unusual child worthy of receiving the title, "The Buddha." He wanted him to enjoy worldly things and be trained only for his role as ruler of his country. The King, therefore, surrounded him with every luxury, provided for his every desire, and sought to protect him from the suffering of the world. When Prince Siddhartha rode outside of the palace grounds the route was always predetermined and the way cleared of every person or thing that might suggest the existence of sickness, old age or death. All diseased and decrepit ones were kept indoors. The young prince grew up in this protected atmosphere, was married to a beautiful princess and for some years was perfectly happy.

But, one day, Prince Siddhartha eluded his protectors and went a different route. He saw a sick man groaning by the side of the road; he saw also a very old man who appeared to be dying; he saw poverty and suffering. He was shocked and inquired of Channa, his servant, how this could be so. Thenceforth he pondered the riddle of men living sensually, carelessly, heedlessly, in a world teeming with sickness and decay and the evidences of death. He became downcast and miserable because now everywhere he saw signs of change and decay. He saw that men grew old, sickened and died. He became possessed with the idea that he should free mankind from this cycle of suffering.

The next time Siddhartha left the palace grounds he met a monk who wore the simple robe of a religious order and carried a begging bowl. Siddhartha noticed that the monk's eyes were clear and untroubled, his face serene and restful. He was told that this religious brother had renounced the world, had no desires and was not fettered by ambition, a man who gave his life to seeking enlightenment.

Now the prince saw what he must do. He gave up his royal heritage and set aside his jewels and rich clothing. He left his wife and family to become a monk with a begging bowl, a seeker of enlightenment. He even gave up food that he might mortify the body and live in the Spirit, but he found that this, also, was not the answer. Finally, through meditation, he found the Enlightenment; he melted into the ocean of Oneness. He saw a vision of mankind freed from the prison of the senses, his soul delivered from the bonds of delusion. He experienced the peace of the Absolute. Siddhartha Gautama became the Buddha, which means the Enlightened One.

Thenceforth he gave his life to teaching mankind how to live. He taught the middle path, the path of self-control, the path that leads to understanding, wisdom and peace. He laid down the doctrine of the Eightfold Path of Virtue which was to remain at the heart of the Buddhist moral teaching forever afterward. The Eightfold Path is:

1. Right belief
2. Right resolve
3. Right speech
4. Right behavior
5. Right occupation
6. Right effort
7. Right contemplation
8. Right concentration

Gautama, the Buddha, discovered that each person had to experience the vicissitudes of life in order to find understanding and right living. He found that it was not wise to protect people from life, that each person must find his own areas of growth in order to ultimately experience the bliss of Oneness. His great teaching came through meditation.

Meditating on Symbols

Some people meditate by concentrating on the flame of a candle. Others observe a talisman in order to go into deep meditation. Some meditate upon their breathing, some picture a beautiful scene, a sunrise or sunset or a peaceful lake to find the peace that leads to meditation. A little later we will tell you the story of a friend of ours who had an instantaneous healing by meditating on a rose bush.

Group Meditation

Group meditation resembles a Quaker Meeting where any number of people sit in the Silence contributing to the high spiritual consciousness of the group. No one breaks the Silence until he feels led by the Spirit to do so. The Spirit of God conducts the meeting, and great spiritual uplift is felt by everyone present.

Today, many church youth groups meditate by sitting on the floor in a circle with the lights out, a candle burning in the center. They, like the Quakers, speak only as inspired by the Spirit within. It is their custom to conclude the meditation by softly singing Jill Jackson's lovely song, "Let There Be Peace On Earth and Let It Begin With Me."

When we have our Universal House of Prayer Meeting at the Abundant Living Foundation, we also sit in a circle and speak as inspired from within. Thus we are able to raise a high spiritual consciousness to which people throughout the world may turn for help in time of need.

Meditation a Deux

Normally we think of meditation as a solitary thing but those who share a great deal in consciousness are able to meditate together. At our house, we often meditate together before meals, before we go to bed at night and whenever the two of us can be alone. We are so in tune that when one of us is led to speak, we find that we are actually thinking the same thing at the same time.

Meditating in the Midst of Confusion

It is commonly believed that one must seek out some quiet place in which to meditate, but not everyone has this opportunity. It is possible to meditate in the midst of confusion.

A man sits in a chair. His eyes are closed. He is very still. But, he is not alone. He is sitting in a board of director's meeting. He is chairman of the board of a large British corporation. J. Arthur Rank moved through his days, even in the midst of great excitement and turmoil, in a meditative way. Noted for his ability to go right to the core of a problem, even when he appeared to be sleeping, he was never caught up in the turmoil of the moment. He had learned that through meditation he could open the inner Self wherein lay his strength.

A friend of mine was a member of the Pacific Coast Stock Exchange and traded on the floor. Those of you who have visited the floor of a stock exchange will know what I mean when I say that this is the height of noise and confusion. My friend told me that he had learned to momentarily go within and meditate on peace. Right in the midst of noise and confusion he would find his inner peace. *Peace* was his mantra. He would emerge from his brief meditation calm and refreshed. He had learned to escape into Reality through the joy of meditation.

Capture and Use Those Wasted Moments for Meditation

Years ago, there was an article in the Reader's Digest about a man whose occupation required that he spend hours waiting to see his prospective customers. As I recall, he sold law books. Even though he had appointments he was required to wait and wait. This used to irk him. Then he discovered meditation. Now, no time was ever wasted. He delighted in these meditation periods provided by his prospective customers. Once he had overcome his feeling of irritation and frustration through the new-found joy of meditation, his sales increased. As he entered the office of his client, he brought with him an inner peace that was felt and appreciated, a poise that enabled him to make the sale where he might have lost it otherwise.

While most of us do not spend much time in waiting rooms, we can use other odd moments for meditation, in the car, the time waiting for the stop light to change, or, for a long line of traffic to move. You actually can meditate with a part of your mind while driving *but don't close your eyes!* Waiting to be served in restaurants or waiting in the check-out line in the super market provide other golden moments. Stop resisting these seemingly wasted moments. They can be valuable to you.

Cornelia Meets the Rose Lady

We were attending a church convention at the time. As we came to the end of a big, noisy, banquet luncheon, I, (Cornelia) realized that I was scheduled to give the opening meditation for the meeting that would follow. Heavens! I never felt less inspired. It behooved me to go apart and meditate a bit before they called me. But where to go? I could only move to a nearby table that was empty. Trying not to attract any attention, I sat down and began to meditate on a statement I had heard Joel Goldsmith make: *God is all there is and this includes me.* The noise, the babble of conversation, faded farther and farther away. *God is all there is and this includes me.* I was all alone in the Silence until I felt someone slip into the chair beside me. Still I kept my eyes closed until I heard her say softly, "God is all there is and this includes you and me." I couldn't believe it. She had tuned in on my meditation! Thus began a very interesting friendship with Estrellita, so aptly named *little star.* Like the morning star her light had endured through a long, dark night. This is the story she told me. It may seem pretty far out to you. You may believe it, or not, as you choose.

It seems at one time Estrellita had had a serious physical condition that threatened her life. Doctors were unable to help her. She had been to spiritual healers to no avail. Finally, one morning, as she sat in the midst of the housework she was unable to do, dirty dishes everywhere, several weeks' washing piled in a corner, everything a mess, she said she just couldn't take it any longer. It came to her that she had been trying to find her healing on the outside, rushing here and there to find some person to help her, when all the time her help could only be found within — *the kingdom of heaven within.*

And so she closed her eyes, and with one giant leap of faith, surrendered her life to God. She never knew how long she sat there in the Silence, but she experienced the bliss of oneness with God. When she opened her eyes, a very strange thing happened. To her, it actually happened, as real as anything she had ever experienced in her life.

A beautiful rose bush grew right up out of the carpet! It emerged slowly. First a little shoot and then the little plant, one leaf unfolding at a time until it stood about two feet high. She held her breath in silent fascination. And then, a beautiful white rose grew out of the plant. First a bud, then, petal by petal, a gorgeous full-blown blossom. But, that is not all. A Voice spoke to her out of the bush. The Voice said to her: *I am the bush and you are the blossom! I give Life to the blossom! I give beauty to the blossom! I give health to the blossom!* That was all.

Estrellita said she could hardly believe that this was happening to her. But, it was very real. There was the beautiful white rose before her, its fragrance filling the house. *I am the bush and you are the blossom.* She began to meditate on this idea, her eyes fastened on the little round rose hip where the blossom joined the bush. *I give life and health to the blossom!* All of a sudden, she felt a warm glow in her body. It started in her toes and moved up through her legs and knees, her torso, her chest, on up to the top of her head until she felt that she was all aglow. This lasted for several minutes.

And then she realized that she was healed! Healed completely! She felt wonderful. She had more vitality than she had ever known. She wanted to run and shout as the blind man did in the Bible—the man who received his sight. She looked back at the rose and watched it slowly fade away. She felt so full of life, she jumped up and started cleaning her house. When her husband came home that evening the house was shining. The clothes were washed and a delicious dinner was bubbling on the stove. She told him the story and he was as thrilled as she. Everyone who ever heard this story from Estrellita received a blessing. I, too, told it to many friends who received healings and great uplift from it.

Meditation

The Lord is in his holy temple, let all the earth keep silent before him.

The Life of God is whole (holy) and perfect;
let us enter into his temple with thanksgiving.

Silence

*I am the Christ, the son of the living God. I
will never never leave you.*

*The Christ of God is the awareness of God with
us, God in us.*

Silence

*I am the bush and you are the blossom. I am
the vine and you are the branches. I give life to
the branches. I give beauty to the blossom.*

Silence

*I am the way, the truth and the life. Rejoice
in me.*

Silence

Chapter VI

RELAXING INTO
DEEP MEDITATION

Let go and let God has become a sort of by-word to metaphysicians. Do not be confused by this expression. It is not a lazy person's excuse to retreat from life. When we say *let go and let God* we do not mean to give up, nor assume a lethargic, defeated attitude toward life.

What It Means to Let Go and Let God

It means to let go of the past with all of its sorrows and frustrations. It means to let go of all feelings of anxiety and limitation and let the Almighty Power of God express through us with zest and enthusiasm. It means to go within and find our Power, but, having found our guidance, we are supposed to take the necessary human footsteps, as inspired from within, as we let God bring about the manifestation of our goal through us.

With God all things are possible, but God works for us, through us. Sitting in meditation day and night could be a method of running away from our responsibilities. We meditate to receive from the within, but are not meant to sit

50

idly by, waiting for an act of God to solve our problem, or for our supply to rain upon us out of the sky without any action on our part. We are co-workers. We are a very important part of the plan.

Meditation is the Letting Go

Meditation is the first step. Letting go of all anxious striving we listen for the inner guidance which comes to us from the Infinite Intelligence within, the great all-knowing Presence which is able to give us our answers. We are not limited, finite beings struggling alone. *For it is God which worketh in you both to will and to do of his good pleasure.*[1]

"But," you may say, "it all sounds wonderful but how can I stop worrying? How can I turn off my mind and make it stop going around in circles like a squirrel in a cage?"

Now is the time to take dominion. You can do it. I'll tell you how. Relaxation, both mental and physical, is the answer. But, how does one relax? When your conscious mind gives an order to the body, the body must obey. Why? Because the body is controlled by the subconscious mind, and the conscious mind directs the subconscious mind. The following relaxing exercise is taken from our book YOUR NEEDS MET.[2]

[1]Philippians 2:13
[2]Jack and Cornelia Addington, YOUR NEEDS MET, Abundant Living Books, Box 100, San Diego, CA 92138.

Relaxing Meditation

Claim for yourself: *I am relaxed. Every muscle, every cell, every atom of my body is relaxed. I am letting go and letting God direct and maintain my life and affairs. I am resting on the Everlasting Arms. I am taking dominion and giving the following orders to my body:*

My toes are relaxed (flex the toes, tense them, turn them up toward the head and then consciously release and relax them).
My ankles are relaxed (tense the ankles and then consciously relax them).
My calves are relaxed (tense the calves and then consciously relax them).
My knees are relaxed (tense the knees and then consciously relax them).
My thighs are relaxed (tense the thighs and then consciously relax them).
My hips are relaxed (tense the hips and then consciously relax them).
My fingers are relaxed (tense the fingers and then consciously relax them).
My hands are relaxed (tense the hands and then consciously relax them).
My arms are relaxed (tense the arms and then consciously relax them).
My diaphragm is relaxed (tense the diaphragm and then consciously relax it).

Now I am letting my shoulders relax, letting

go of any burden I have been carrying. I am re-laxing my neck muscles (tense them and relax them). I am relaxed. My scalp is relaxed . . . . my head is relaxed . . . my brain is relaxed . . . my mind is relaxed . . . my eyes are relaxed . . . my face is relaxed (let expression go limp) . . . my whole body is relaxed. Now in this relaxed state, I surrender myself to the Perfect Power within me. I realize that all of life continues without my doing anything about it . . . I AM LET-TING GO AND LETTING GOD!

There is Only One Power

It was Emerson who said, *Do the thing and you will have the Power.* Maybe you don't feel filled with peace right this moment. But pretend that you do. Eventually you will find that peace has become your way of life, and out of this peace will come power. Peace is Power. Peace and Power are both synonyms for God. There is only one Power, and that Power is God. Peace, Poise, and Power are attributes of God just as Love and Life are attributes of God. There is no power apart from this universal Power which we all share. This Power is omnipotent. To It nothing is impossible; but, we must be at peace with ourselves and with life before we can make conscious contact with It.

What the world thinks of as power is really energy, force; vibration. Actually all Power is

given to us. We do not manufacture It. We just
use It. If it were not for this Power we would be
as helpless as babes. We use God's omnipotent
Power in the measure that we are able to accept
it. Nothing is too difficult for the person who uses
omnipotent Power.

Peace Comes First

First, we must find peace. Believe it or not, it
is possible to find peace in this complex world.
*Let there be peace on earth and let it begin with
me.*

As the song says, it must begin with us. No one
can thrust it upon us. Little by little, our thinking becomes changed. We learn to trust the Spirit
within for guidance in all that we do. As our own
consciousness is uplifted, our health and circumstances are improved. What happens within becomes out-pictured in the world around us. It all
works for us, *through* us. Do not expect it to be
handed to you from the outside. It doesn't work
that way. The new awareness works from the
within out, transcending our circumstances and
radiating into every part of life.

Did you ever feel that you were lost, lonely and
rejected, unable to cope with the problems con-
fronting you? The truth is that instead of being
alone, confused and unhappy, you are right now
in perfect unity with the Power within which is
peace, poise, and right action in your life and

affairs. There is no reason to think of ourselves as being separated from the *whole* of Life. Life is one and we are one with it. Through meditation we experience this oneness of Life.

So we set out on a wonderful adventure together, seeking peace and knowing that the very peace we are seeking is right within us, expressing in and through us. We seek poise, knowing that Life lives through us without fear or anxiety, for we are outlets of that perfect Life.

The scripture says: *God hath made man upright; but they have sought out many inventions.*[3] Let's be done with those mental inventions that lead only to turmoil. God made man upright, poised, at peace with the world. Let us go within, quietly, serenely, to find that inner poise through the joy of meditation.

Dispelling Chaos and Confusion

We all get caught up in the confusion that results from whirling around too fast on that outer rim of life. Then, we need to go within, to become still and contemplate the inner Peace that is never confused, never in a hurry, never disturbed. It is the Truth of our being. It only awaits our recognition of It. *In returning and rest shall we be saved; in quietness and in confidence shall be our strength.*[4]

[3] Ecclesiastes 7:29
[4] Isaiah 30:15

Nothing can separate us from this Peace within us *unless we let it*. It is only our *responses* to life that get us into trouble. The real Self abides in eternal harmony. It is possible to dwell in that harmony at all times by turning away from the thought of confusion, by refusing to fear things and conditions in the outer world. This is accomplished through meditation.

Each one is a triune being—spirit, mind and body, all so beautifully interrelated that when we relax the body it helps us relax the mind. When the mind is stilled, the spirit can receive from the Universal Mind Power. Understanding this, Jesus said, *all Power is given unto me in heaven* (within) *and in earth* (the outer experience).

Thus it is very important to each one of us to learn to relax the body if we would know the joy of deep meditation.

Practice the relaxation exercises in this chapter until you are able to give the directive command to the body, *I am relaxed,* and have the body respond at once. Here is another meditation to help you relax into meditation. It is also to be found in our book, YOUR NEEDS MET.[5] You will note that in each of these relaxation exercises the first person "I" is used. This is to help you give direction to your subconscious mind. So think to yourself:

[5] Addington, op. cit.

I am Relaxed

Feel your muscles letting go. You are letting go of all tension. Now claim for yourself:

I am completely, perfectly and wholly relaxed. I am letting go right now of every muscle, every nerve, every bone, every tissue in my body. I rest in the knowledge that there is within me an Intelligence which knows how to function my body perfectly, which knows how to function my affairs perfectly, which knows how to function my life perfectly. I let the Intelligence within me tell me what to do and how to do it. I move easily through life, doing the right thing at exactly the right time. I am free from any irritation. I am in perfect harmony with life. Nothing irritates me. No person annoys me. I do not condemn myself. I have no anxiety for the future. I surrender my every action; my every demand; my every fear, worry, anxiety, and burden to God within me whom I worship and adore. I trust God to care for me, knowing that divine right action is operating in all of my affairs. I am completely relaxed in God.

Silence

Chapter VII

LETTING GO WITH BALANCE

There are as many routes to meditation as there are ways to pray effectively. Each one must find his own path, the way that feels right to him. In the Silence, the Power is released to do the mighty works.

When we feel that we have difficult decisions to make, insurmountable tasks looming up ahead of us, then it is time to walk away from our tensions and go within to find the Peace wherein the Power lies.

Is There a Difference Between Prayer and Meditation?

We are often asked, "What is the difference between prayer and meditation?" Actually, there is very little difference. In meditation, we contemplate the God Power within, recognizing that it is All-Power, All-Intelligence, All-Life, everywhere present. Joyfully we commune with the Power, identifying ourselves in Its image and likeness.

In scientific prayer, we may take a more overt

step by letting our needs be known, or "choosing our good" is the way it is often put. However, actually, our desires are always known to the deep mind, so this is only a matter of organizing our own thinking. As we contemplate the Infinite, becoming one with Its majesty, we align ourselves with all that It is and let the Power flow through us into manifestation. So, you see, it is really hard to say where meditation leaves off and prayer begins. Every meditation is a form of prayer.

Common to both prayer and meditation is a secret ingredient that must be present if the work is to be effective. It is the difference between praying aright and praying amiss, the difference between spiritual meditation and simply brooding about a problem. The secret ingredient is *release*. Every step we take in our meditation is for the purpose of bringing us to this point, that place in consciousness where we are able to "let go and let God" with perfect trust. Meditating on the Power within is for the purpose of recognizing the Great Potential lying within us that is able to do all things for us, through us. As we are able to unify with It, we go a step further toward the ultimate goal — complete release.

Exchanging Weakness for Power

It was once our privilege to meditate with a teacher from Wakefield, Massachusetts, Mr. Newton Dillaway, a true mystic. He had come to conduct a mid-week meditation meeting. The meeting generally lasted an hour, but this one went on for three hours, to everyone's amazement. The time went so fast. Half of this time was spent in the Silence, the most moving Silence we had ever experienced. Mr. Dillaway taught us a way of meditation never to be forgotten, one that we have passed on to others ever since. Now we are going to share it with you.

This is a meditation that is apt to mark a turning point in your life. It could provide you with a dramatic spiritual experience every time you use it. You could find it a particularly effective meditation that could enable you to release even the most stubborn kind of problem. It is divided into two parts: first, the releasing; second, the accepting.

Allow at least a half hour for this meditation, more if possible.

Part I: The Releasing

During the first half of the meditation, you are to release all that has troubled you. It is a cleansing of the subconscious mind, evacuating the troublesome thoughts that have, in the past, interfered with your happiness, peace of mind, and accomplishment. This is the way it is done: Think to the self:

I Am Letting Go With Balance

Just a word of explanation: Letting go with balance is quite different from letting go without balance. Were you ever on the high end of a teeter-totter when the person on the other end jumped off? It was quite a letdown, wasn't it? You went boom! When we let go with balance, we are upheld in perfect balance by the almighty Power of God. No matter how many ups and downs we have experienced in the past, now we are in balance, upheld by infinite Intelligence, omnipotent Power. We rest on the everlasting arms. In short, we are in perfect balance. We are letting go to the Perfect Power within to which all things are possible. So, with a feeling of perfect balance, trusting in the Power within, we are going to let go of every problem. And now, we individualize our meditation by taking our worrisome thoughts, our uneasy feelings, our fears and misgivings, and letting them go with balance.

I am letting go with balance.

Silence

I am letting go with balance.

Silence

I am letting go with balance.

Silence

Your personal meditation might go something like this:

I am letting go of the fear of meeting strangers; I am letting go with balance. I am letting go of all uneasiness about my financial future; I am letting go with balance. I am letting go of the personality problems at my office; I am letting go with balance. I am letting go of all concern about my health and the health of my wife; I am letting go with balance.

When you have released every problem you can possibly think of, you will have a beautiful sense of freedom, as if you were lighter than air. You will be floating on a cloud, blissfully free, at last. Even if you were to stop here you would be greatly benefitted by your meditation.

But, do not stop here. Let us sit in the Silence and revel in this new-found freedom.

Silence

I am letting go with balance.

Silence

I am letting go with balance.

Silence

I am letting go with balance.

Silence

Now we are ready for the second part.

Part II: The Accepting

Now, you are cleansed. You have emptied every problem out of your subconscious mind and are ready to be filled. Life abhors a vacuum and will rush in to fill the empty places. This part of the meditation is based on II Corinthians 9:8. It is a verse you will want to call to memory often.

And God is able to make all grace abound toward you; that ye, always having all sufficiency in all things, may abound to every good work.

God is able.

Silence

God is able.

Silence

God is able.

Silence

And your personal meditation would go something like this:

"God is able to meet strangers with complete aplomb. God is able to heal every human problem. God is able to provide for each of His children as the need arises—before they call I will answer. God is able to express perfect health. God is able!"

God is able.

Silence

God is able.

Silence

God is able.

Silence

You do not have to relate the *God is able* to your outer affairs. The quotation is to be used as a mantra until you feel the Power stirring within you. The longer you continue the Silence the better you will feel.

Now you are free, indeed. You have let go of the past and accepted your highest good. You are forever and ever in balance with Life. God is able and you can relax, release and rejoice!

Chapter VIII

MEDITATION FOR
SPIRITUAL UNFOLDMENT

The Spirit within us is like a fountain of pure spiritual consciousness out of which flows all Wisdom, all Joy, all Goodness. Nothing that anyone does or says, or fails to do or say, can take away that Joy that comes from within.

> *The will of God for you at this very moment is something joyous, something beautiful and thrillingly interesting, and, in fact, far beyond anything that you could possibly sit down and wish for with your conscious mind*, wrote Emmet Fox.

The Bible tells us that no gift can be received unless it first comes from the Spirit. That is why you can read all the books, hear all the spiritual teachers and still not become spiritually illumined until you receive the Truth from the Spirit within.

When we commune, as we do in deep meditation, with the will of God for us, we are open and receptive to receive an awareness of the divine potential within us. As we sit quietly in the Silence, the Truth begins to well up within us as spiritual

unfoldment. Through meditation Truth is un-
folded in such a personal way that it means something special to us. We can no longer doubt. As
Ernest Holmes used to say, *we know and we know
that we know.*

The Unfoldment of Spiritual Consciousness Through Meditation

The first step in spiritual unfoldment is the
recognition of God's handiwork in the world in
which we live. As Moses said when he beheld the
burning bush that did not consume itself: *I will
now turn aside, and see this great sight.* Once we
take time to turn aside and take a look at the
glorious cloud effects, those fabulous sunsets, the
intricate designs and flamboyant colors of nature,
we must concede that the Master Artist is constantly at work expressing Himself in all of life.
With this recognition comes a great surge of joy.

The second step brings even greater joy as we
become aware of the Mind of God in us. Using
that Mind *which was also in Christ Jesus,* we find
God through meditation. It is in the Silence that
we are able to understand abstractions. God is
not visible to the human eye which sees only the
effects, but the divine *I Am* within us knows God
intimately. *I am the way, the truth, and the life:
no man cometh unto the Father, but by me.*[1] It is

[1] St. John 14:6

through the Christ mind, discovered in the Silence, that we come to know God and believe that He exists.

The third step is the feeling of the Presence. It is built into us, but only as we go within does it become meaningful. As we act upon this awareness of the Presence, trust It, love It, follow Its guidance, we begin to live the spiritual life into manifestation. With this great step forward, we overcome fear and apprehension. Now we can lean back on those everlasting arms and trust Life to live Itself through us in Its perfect way.

When Jesus shocked the Jews by telling them *I and my Father are one,*[2] he had this realization of his union with the Father. It was the end of the search for him. Whatever followed was the will of the Father and could only be for good. To his fellow Jews who lived by the law and not by the Spirit, this was blasphemy. And so they took up stones to stone him. The literal-minded deceive themselves. *God is not a man*[3] to be limited by human qualities. But, we put off our humanhood when we discover, through meditation, the Perfect Power within. Then we are able to say with Jesus, *all Power is given unto me in heaven* (within) *and in earth* (the outer.)[4] This is the joy of meditation. Nothing can ever defeat us again.

[2]St. John 10:30
[3]Numbers 23:19
[4]Matthew 28:18

The Unknown God

When Paul came to Athens, he was greatly disturbed to find the city completely given over to idolatry. The men of Athens took him to Mars' Hill, an open place where the court convened and where philosophers met to discuss all subjects. There he told them his concept of God.

> *Then certain philosophers of the Epicureans, and of the Stoics, encountered him. And some said, What will this babbler say? others, He seemeth to be a setter forth of strange gods; because he preached unto them Jesus, and the resurrection. And they took him, and brought him unto Areopagus, saying, May we know what this new doctrine, whereof thou speakest is? For thou bringest certain strange things to our ears; we would know therefore what these things mean. (For all the Athenians and strangers which were there spent their time in nothing else, but either to tell, or to hear some new thing).* [5]

They were not too different from us, were they? And we, too, would welcome Paul in to give us some light in expanding our concept of God. Let's hear what he had to say:

> *Then Paul stood in the midst of Mars'*

[5] Acts 17:18-21

Hill, and said, Ye men of Athens, I perceive that in all things ye are too superstitious. For as I passed by, and beheld your devotions, I found an altar with this inscription, TO THE UNKNOWN GOD. Whom therefore ye ignorantly worship, him declare I unto you. God that made the world, and all things therein, seeing that he is Lord of heaven and earth, dwelleth not in temples made with hands; Neither is worshipped with men's hands, as though he needed any thing, seeing he giveth to all life, and breath, and all things; And hath made of one blood all nations of men for to dwell on all the face of the earth, and hath determined the times before appointed, and the bounds of their habitation; That they should seek the Lord, if haply they might feel after him, and find him, though he be not far from every one of us; For in him we live, and move, and have our being; as certain also of your own poets have said, For we are also his offspring. For as much then as we are the offspring of God, we ought not to think that the Godhead is like unto gold, or silver, or stone, graven by art and man's device.[6]

Paul carried on the concept that Jesus expressed: *God is Spirit.*

[6]Acts 17:22–29

The Known God

Each one of us has his own concept of God. Your concept of God is your God. God is Infinite, and through meditation we expand our awareness of the Infinite. God, being all-Power, all-Intelligence, all-Love, everywhere present, withholds nothing from us. It is therefore highly important that we expand our awareness of Him, pushing out the horizons of our awareness in ever-widening circles.

Paul, who believed in one God and Father of all *Who is above all, and through all, and in you all,*[7] said: *My God shall supply all your needs according to his riches in glory by Christ Jesus.*[8] He did not mean that he had some special claim to God. He simply meant to say, The God that I believe in supplies my daily need, manna for today, constant protection just when I need it, a very present help in time of trouble for me; working through the Christ, the Spirit within, as He worked through Jesus. This God that I trust will supply all your needs, too.

There is an old saying, "When you define God, you lose God." *"Un Dieu define est un Dieu fini,"* says the old French proverb. I disagree. This fallacy comes from an oriental idea that the only way to define God is to say what God is not, the assumption being that any time you say what God

[7] Ephesians 4:6
[8] Phillippians 4:19

is, you are limiting the Infinite. Jesus did not hesitate to tell the woman of Samaria at Jacob's well that *God is Spirit.* He called God the Father, and described Him as being like a loving father. *Behold the fowls of the air; for they sow not, neither do they reap, nor gather into barns; yet your heavenly Father feedeth them. Are ye not much better than they?*[9]

The Kingdom is at Hand

There has been a great deal of superstition about God and His kingdom. Somewhere, somehow, man conceived the idea that the heaven which he sought was a place, a city paved with gold, where he might live a life of ease in the far-distant future. He thought he had to sweat this life out, put up with all sorts of inconveniences and discomforts, that he might earn a ticket to this distant paradise. Had this been true, would not Jesus have told his followers where this place was? No, he told them that heaven was to be enjoyed now. He said, *The kingdom of God is within you . . . The kingdom of heaven is at hand.*[10] He taught that the kingdom of God is a consciousness of God-given dominion over the things of this world. It was to be attained, and is attained today, by repenting, which simply means, the changing of the mind.

[9]Matthew 6:26
[10]Luke 17:21; Matthew 4:17

The kingdom of God is still at hand. It is ours the moment we put aside our old foolish concepts and realize that God is right within us, expressing through us. Through His mighty Power, we are heirs to the kingdom today.

God is in Us

Now is the appointed time. If God is to be found within us, what shall we look for? It is impossible to completely define God, but with persistence, man can gain a larger and larger concept of the Infinite. Let's see what we do know about God. The Bible tells us, *God is not a man.*[11] The poet Tennyson, said, *God is All in All, Omnipresent,* which means everywhere present in the same degree, Infinite. Therefore, God is within us and within all of life, binding it all together in one perfect whole.

We know from the Bible that God is Spirit, *God is Spirit and they that worship him must worship him in Spirit and in truth.*[12] *God is love, and he that dwelleth in love dwelleth in God and God in him.*[13] Could anything be clearer? God is the Spirit of Love within us which, when recognized and called forth, becomes omnipotent Power, the Perfect Power within us.

God is light, and in him is no darkness at all.[14]

---

[11]Numbers 23:19   [12]St. John 4:24
[13]I John 4:16   [14]I John 1:5

If God is all there is, everywhere present, how then can there be darkness (ignorance) in our lives? Light means understanding, Truth, divine illumination. As Emerson said, *There is one mind common to all individual men. Every man is an inlet to the same and to all the same.* We discover this contact with the Infinite through the joy of meditation.

Plato spoke of God as Divine Mind. The Light shines through the one Mind, dispelling the darkness. Each one is an inlet to the divine Mind and an outlet of the divine Mind which is all-knowing. Emerson went on to say, *What Plato has thought, you may think; what a saint has felt, you may feel. Who hath access to the universal mind is a party to all that is or can be done.* It is all yours through meditation. Take time to meditate. It is well worth it.

Meditation

Let us meditate on the thought:

I love the Life of God within me.

Quietly we turn from the problems and the cares of the day and think to ourselves:

I love the Life of God within me.

Silence

God is the only Power and the only Presence. I am a divine, perfect, spiritual being,

forever one with my Source.
I love the Life of God within me.

Silence

I love the Life of God within me.
I love the Life of God around me.
I love the Life of God in everyone.
I love the Life of God everywhere present.

Silence

I love the Life of God within me.
I am one with the Life of God.
All of Life loves me.
I am immersed in God's Love.
I melt into the Oneness of Life.

Silence

Chapter IX

LET HIM WHO HAS EARS HEAR

Of all the joys of meditation, a well-developed sense of intuition is the most precious. Once we have learned to open the inner door through meditation, this valuable aid to joyous living comes welling up within us when we least expect it, a sort of guardian angel watching over us and coming swiftly to our assistance when we need it most.

He that hath an ear, let him hear what the spirit saith to the churches.[1] The churches are the spiritually illumined thoughts within the individual and the aggregate spiritual illumination of the many who are open to receive intuition. To *the churches* (our own spiritual receptivity) it comes from some vast reservoir of inner knowing.

Intuition is Something You Can Use

There is that within *you* which knows. It knows all that you need to know, now and forever. It communicates with you freely once you have opened the way through meditation. Do not expect it to interrupt your meditation, although

[1]Revelation 2:7

75

it sometimes does. Sometimes it speaks to you in a dream, at other times you may be awakened with the wisdom that you seek. It comes *as you need it,* once you have opened that inner door.

The Awakening to Intuition

In his book THE SECRET PATH, Paul Brunton wrote that it is possible *to catch the mind like a bird in a net, its constant flight stopped, its restless activity quiet,* and that once this was accomplished we were then ready for the next step — *the awakening to intuition.* He brings out that intuition is unsleeping, always ready, but that it is man who is asleep and needs to be awakened to his inner potential.

The student who is willing to go apart and practice meditation soon finds that Truth is not just a revelation reserved for the guru, but that it dwells within each one. It has always been there but now he is able to call it forth. Having retreated from the bustle and confusion of the outer world, he becomes receptive to the inner Voice.

The invisible potential awaits us: *Behold, I stand at the door and knock: if any man hear my voice, and open the door, I will come in to him, and will sup with him, and he with me.*[2] The door opens from within. Universal Truth awaits each one, standing patiently at the door of consciousness. When we open that inner door

[2]Revelation 3:20

through meditation, the divine awareness will come in and share with us. No one ever said it better than the immortal Robert Browning:

Truth is within ourselves; it takes no rise
From outward things whate'er you may believe.
There is an inmost centre in us all,
Where truth abides in fullness; and to know
Rather consists in opening out a way
Whence the imprisoned splendor may escape,
Than in effecting entry for a light
Supposed to be without.

People meditate for various reasons, but our highest goal should be that we may receive Truth from the Teacher within which Jesus called the *Spirit of Truth . . . for he dwelleth with you, and shall be in you . . . he shall teach you all things*[3] When we meditate we are able to receive directly from the Divine Source. Meditation is our contact with spiritual consciousness. It is our link with the Divine. Meditation is not only mind expanding, it is our contact with the Infinite and therefore the possibilities are infinite. Meditation, in time, could lead to Cosmic Consciousness.

The Mystics Live By Intuition

To the mystic, intuition is a way of life. But, who are the mystics? Are you a mystic?

Today the word *mystic* is often used wrongly.

[3]St. John 14:17,26

Television personalities use the word to designate anyone who is different, a soothsayer, a magician, or a psychic medium. Actually they are going far afield. Our dictionary defines *mysticism: a spiritual discipline aiming at union with the divine through meditation.*

Ernest Holmes gave us a good definition:

> *A mystic is not a mysterious person but is one who has a deep, inner sense of Life and of his unity with the Whole. Mysticism and psychism are entirely different. One is real while the other may, or may not be an illusion.*
>
> *A mystic is one who intuitively perceives Truth and, without mental process, arrives at spiritual realization. It is from the teaching of the great mystics that the best in the philosophy of the world has come. Who was there who could have taught such men as these? By what process of mentality did they arrive at their profound conclusions? We are compelled to recognize that Spirit alone was their Teacher; they were indeed taught of God.*
>
> *Our great religions have been given by a few who climbed the heights of spiritual vision and caught a fleeting glimpse of Ultimate Reality. No living soul could have taught them what they knew.* [4]

[4] Ernest Holmes, SCIENCE OF MIND, (Dodd, Mead & Co., New York, N.Y., 1938)

Ernest Holmes himself was a mystic. He often told me how much he depended upon the Inspiration he received directly from the divine Source through meditation.

Intuition as a Practical Help

Suppose you need an answer, an idea, a solution that eludes you. Start by knowing that the answer lies within you. Meditate. The Divine Knower within has all of the answers. The All-knowing is right where you are. Being Omnipresent, it has to include you. All that God is is right within you. It is the Truth of your own being; *the Spirit of truth within you which will teach you all that you need to know.* As a moth is drawn to the light, so must you be drawn to that inner Light that has the answers you seek. As you meditate, something wonderful happens— the problem fades away and you emerge from your meditation with a sense of fulfillment. The answer will come at the right time. It will all seem so right, so simple, you may not recognize it for the miracle it is.

The Still, Small Voice

Have you heard the *still, small voice,* that powerful voice from within that sometimes thunders in the Silence? It comes to us when we are willing to be quiet enough to listen. Sometimes it is more like a movement of the mind coming

forth as an idea or direction needed. Sometimes
it is a feeling thing, but, like a voice, it is heard
on the spiritual level.

When you hear the *still, small voice* you know
that the Spirit has spoken. Sometimes it sounds
like a human voice magnified by many echo
chambers. At other times it is more of a lilting
surge of the Spirit, lifting us up and setting us
free. Such was the recent experience of one of my
correspondents. She said that she and her husband
had had a number of problems to overcome. But,
one morning as she stood at the stove preparing
breakfast, a *voice* said to her, *"God will take care
of you."* She was surprised. For once she had not
been thinking about her problems. Her whole
attention had been given to what she was doing.
Something happened to her when the *voice* spoke
to her. The wonderful thing was that it brought
her a lasting peace, entering into every activity.
"Now," she wrote, "I do not feel that I need to be
concerned about anything as long as I keep my
trust in the Power within remembering *God will
take care of you."*

One day at a luncheon meeting of a service
club a man sitting next to me told me this inci-
dent. It seems that the night before he had attended a meeting in Los Angeles and was driving
south on a through street. It was about eleven
o'clock at night. There was little traffic. All of a
sudden a voice, which seemed to fill him and the
car, shouted, *"Bill, STOP!"* When he heard

his name, he was suddenly alerted. At the word, *STOP,* he slammed on the brakes. Seconds later a car passed in front of his car, missing it by inches. Had he not put on the brakes exactly when he did, he would have been involved in a collision. Bill said he pulled to the curb and sat quietly for a few moments. A great sense of peace came over him, a feeling of great protection. He thought about the experience but was not the least bit afraid. The feeling of peace persisted. He said that the voice was so strong that it was just as if someone had been sitting in the car. There was no one visible. And yet . . .

What do these stories have in common? In each case there was an urgent need, a sense of release to the omnipotent Power through prayer and then . . . that *still, small voice* that shouts in the Silence, followed by a deep sense of peace and protection.

Sometimes The Voice Speaks to Us in Dreams

Intuition is a divine gift that has seldom been understood. We do not hear it as often as we should, because we so seldom take time to listen for it, or to ask it for answers.

Two stories come to mind that illustrate this point. Recently, I was awakened from a deep sleep. As I struggled up to the surface of consciousness, I heard the melodious tone of Boots Randolph playing the saxophone. The tune was:

"When The Saints Come Marching In." The music in my mind became louder and louder as if it was determined to wake me completely. When I fully awoke, the tune was ringing in my ears. Then it came to me. Several days earlier I had been playing that record on our stereo record player. Then Something said to me, *"Go and check your stereo unit. You left it on."* The little red light did not show in the daylight. I had to be awakened in the night hours in order to see it. What a cute way God has of telling us things!

A friend of ours purchased an evening gown for a special occasion. As the long-awaited date drew near, she went to her closet to check on the dress. Did it need altering? Were her shoes the right color? etc. The dress was not to be found. She looked. And looked. She could not find the dress. Finally, as the date drew closer, she was desperate. She finally stopped trying to do it all by herself and asked the infinite Intelligence to help her. That night she went to sleep in peace. She had shifted the responsibility. In the middle of the night she was awakened out of a deep sleep. As she lay there wondering why she had been literally shaken out of her best sleep of the night, the *still, small voice* spoke to her. Gently, at first, then more and more insistently. *"Go and look in your closet,"* it told her. "But, I have," she replied. *"Look again,"* the voice argued, *"Look in the very bottom of your garment bag."* Sure enough, she looked in the bottom of the garment bag. It was dark down there. And there it was, a soft little fluff of chiffon that she would never have seen otherwise.

Dream Symbols

My wife has recently been concerned about our computer programming. "There must be a way to work this out," she told me. "God is able to perfect it, I know."

"Be Thou our program director," she prayed.

At three o'clock in the morning she awoke with a start. "I won't! I won't" she cried, sitting up in bed.

"What won't you do?" I asked her. And then she laughed. "I dreamed that the computer told me that I must put my hair up on rollers three times, each time on a different set of rollers, and that each time I must be sure that every hair was in the exact sequence of the first time!"

She thought a few moments. "I get the message," she said, laughing. "Everything we do on our computer has to be printed out on three different kinds of paper. This is a fantastic amount of work for the office staff. Each time it prints out in the exact alphabetical sequence.

"But, *we really don't have to do it three times.* I'm sure there is a way to get three-part paper so that we can print it only once and have the same result." There it was. The message was loud and clear. But it came when she was quiet enough to hear it, quiet enough to get the symbolism of

the dream. It came in a way that she could understand and get the message. What could be more
tiresome and time-consuming than curling her
hair three times in a row! Something must be
done to overcome extra computer work. Something *could* be done to save the extra work in
the office. Our programmer worked it out so that
the job had to be done only once.

You've heard of *woman's intuition.* Intuition
is not something that has been reserved for women
only. This divine faculty is available just as read-
ily to men. Now is the time for all of us to start
using it!

Intuition, a Most Valuable Tool

Every idea person has learned to rely upon the
unseen Mind to which he has direct contact. He
uses INTUITION, the most valuable tool man
has. Intuition is also called direct knowing, or
divine guidance. Mystics call it *showings;* reli-
gionists, *leadings.* The ancients spoke of *illumina-
tions.* Inventors have *ideas.*

When ideas well up from deep within us, seemingly out of nowhere, we are using intuition.
Intuition is *knowledge based upon insight, or
spiritual perception, rather than on reasoning.*
Intuition can be an immediate answer to prayer
in time of need. It is the *still, small voice* the
Bible refers to. It is the idea that comes un-
announced after you have given up the whole
project as a loss.

Intuition does not arise deliberately, but spontaneously; not voluntarily, but involuntarily. It can never be coerced. It is like an unexpected voice that comes at the precise moment when it is needed. Sometimes it bids us renounce what we have been doing; sometimes it brings us a sudden alteration of outlook, judgment or decision. It is the most valuable thing in our lives, if we will heed it. The truly successful man or woman is the one who has learned to listen to the voice of intuition and follow its guidance.

Intuition is Sublime Inspiration

Intuition in its highest sense is sublime inspiration which comes through to us when we are able to get the human self out of the way. As Pitirim Sirokin puts it: *It transcends ego entirely and unconditionally.* It must have been in a flash of divine intuition that Jesus said, *Of mine own self I can do nothing, the Father that dwelleth in me he doeth the works.*[5] It was Browning's *inner splendor,* St. Theresa's *not me, but God working through me.* To Moses and the Israelites, it was *the pillar of fire by night and the cloud by day.*

Every mystic knew that the little self must die before the divine Self can come through in all Its glory. As one consciously centers himself in the formless Presence of God and becomes responsive only to that which is Good, two things

[5]St. John 5:30; 14:10

will happen: he will begin to feel the Presence
of God, and he will emerge with some definite
guidance or leading.

One of our great teachers, Frederick Keeler,
at the turn of the century called this guidance
direct knowing. It has been said, *When we talk
to God, that is prayer: when God talks to us, that
is inspiration*. It is the voice of intuition that
speaks to us in the Silence.

Intuition is the most valuable asset that man
has. Plotinus said that it is a thing that all men
possess but few use. Through intuition man learns
more than through any other avenue of knowledge. We labor to learn things through books
and lectures and other means, but through intuition we can cut right through to the Source.

So the next time you need some wisdom, do
not run hither and yon, asking friends and neigh-
bors what you should do. Sit quietly in the Silence
and invoke the infinite Wisdom of God. Think
to yourself: *Divine Intelligence within me knows
the answer*. And then sit quietly in a relaxed and
peaceful frame of mind and anticipate that answer. It may not come then, but it will come—
perhaps when you are doing something else at a
later time—but, through meditation, you will
have opened the door in Mind to receive the
answer that you seek.

Meditation

Now we are ready to open that inner door . . .
Let us start as the Eastern mystics do, by asking,

"Who am I?"

Who am I?

Silence

Who am I?

Silence

(Now in the Silence listen while the Spirit speaks to you).

You are the Light that God shines through.
You are the place where God speaks to you.
You are the ear that hears God speak.

Silence

Speak, Lord, thy servant heareth!

Silence

Now, just listen. Do not be impatient. It will come.

Silence

Chapter X

MEDITATION PUTS US IN TUNE WITH THE INFINITE

Ralph Waldo Trine wrote a book that is now a classic. Just thinking of the title does something for us — IN TUNE WITH THE INFINITE. When we are in tune with the Infinite, we are consciously one with God. Only then are we able to let the Infinite flow through us into perfect expression. How, then, do we go about getting ourselves in tune? Since to be in tune is the ultimate goal of spiritual living, is there a way to be sure that we *are* in tune? Yes, there is. It is through meditation. There is nothing we can do that is so important to us. These are memorable moments.

A Memorable Meditation

Through deep meditation we agree with the Life of God and become consciously one with It. I will always remember a certain meditation of mine with a feeling of joy. It stands out in my mind as a high spot in my spiritual journey. On this occasion I was in deep meditation for several hours. Out of this meditation came such inspiration that I feed upon it to this day. I have only to recall the peace, the glow, the deep harmony of that morning to live in it again, as one would go back and walk again through a fragrant rose garden and feel once more the warmth of the sun and smell the flowers and again be in harmony with life. It was more a feeling thing than words, but out of it came one very important word— AGREEMENT.

Agreement

What does the word *agree* mean? It means to harmonize with; to work together; to be unified with; to be as one. When two agree, they are as one. When there is agreement consciously and subconsciously within the individual, he is unified within himself and with all of Life. The Perfect Power is released to flow through him into accomplishment.

How does one let agreement come into his life? In the world of effects, the material or physical level of life, there are many happenings that cause us to become inwardly disturbed if we let them. It is still our God-given prerogative to choose how we shall react to the effects of life.

The Perfect Power within is never touched by outer conditions. From It comes peace and harmony and divine right action in the midst of chaos. *There am I in the midst of you*[1] is always the turning point.

The entire teaching of Jesus had to do with

[1]Matthew 18:20

agreement, bringing man into a sense of harmony and oneness with Life, where there are no judgments or hostilities, and all is ruled by love. Agreement is a very real thing. God and I are a majority. God and the *I AM* of anyone are a majority. It makes no difference how many there may be who disagree, who are in contention, or who are striving and struggling against the one.

Divine Intelligence His to Use

All power is given unto me in heaven (within) *and earth* (the outer), said Jesus, because he knew that the Christ Self was the individualized life of God within himself. This made divine Intelligence his to use, and the Power was used by him for mighty works. He did not need to waste time resisting the conditions around him because he had all Power within himself, and with this Power he could overcome any obstacle, even death itself. It is through this awareness that we find the perfect response to the actions that take place around us today.

This, then, is the answer—agreement with the Perfect Power within, letting It live through us, healing us of hatred, judgments and resentments; letting It guide and instruct us in the way that we should go, taking all resistance out of our everyday living, giving us freedom to live creatively and happily in any situation, giving us the Power and the Intelligence to reconstruct our lives into paths of peace and divine right action.

Non-Resistance

Having meditated at length on this subject, I find that deep meditation on agreement will release Power in an individual's life which will overcome or neutralize resistance. Resistance is probably the number one enemy of mankind. If you will look back in your life, you will find that any failure, disease, and discord which you have experienced has always been rooted in a sense of resistance or separation from Life. Perhaps you blamed these unhappy experiences on someone else, but that in itself was resistance and did not help you rid yourself of your misery.

Resistance, at the time, always seems so logical to the human mind, which fails to realize it is dealing with poison. Contrariwise, the healing power of agreement is the way out of any difficulty. When we look away from the object of resistance and focus our attention in meditation on the Perfect Power within, new channels of creativity are opened to us.

When there is no resistance, there will be no antagonistic people in our experience. Resistance is the antipathy of agreement. It is the thing we have to watch out for more than anything else in our lives—resisting our circumstances, resisting the people in our experience, resisting conditions, even resisting the weather.

Let's find something good to build on in every situation. This is a wonderful way to rule out that old enemy resistance. Find the good and praise it. Voice no criticism nor condemnation. Meditate daily on agreement. Try it for a week and you will find that you have opened up the way to creativity. All the channels are open. Nothing stands in your way. Now God can live through you into an expression of health and well-being such as you had not believed possible.

Even so-called incurable diseases can be healed through practicing agreement. I once knew a woman who was healed of terminal cancer when she meditated on agreement. She said she got rid of her *little hates* as she called them. Resistance to washing the dishes was one of them. Ask yourself: "Are my resistances worth keeping?" Agree with Life and Life will agree with you. Agree with the Perfect Power within you and it will perfect all that concerns you.

Man's Extremity is God's Opportunity

Surrender to God is the beginning of agreement with Life. A man by the name of John Flavel, back in 1690 said it first:

Man's extremity is God's opportunity.

Since that time, many others have found this truth and claimed it for their own. It is when we are faced with our greatest need that we turn at last to the great Power within and finally agree with it. We find, in looking back into history, that some of the most creative periods in man's

existence were in times of great stress and turmoil, such as during a war or some other time of
crisis. When man is faced with an emergency he
is more inclined to trust the Power than at any
other time. Perhaps it is because at such a time
he realizes his own inadequacy and is forced to
reach out to the Power that is greater than he is.

A Sense of Separation

Until we are in agreement with the Perfect
Power, we are in conflict and this conflict causes
us to have a feeling of separation from Life. Some
doctors say that many of our ills come from stress.
Stress is conflict or lack of agreement with Life.
The Perfect Power within is able and willing to
bring us back into perfect harmony with Life
when we are willing to turn to It. It is easy to see
that any great challenge that forces us to turn,
even out of a sense of desperation, to the Perfect
Power that is all Power, agreeing with It at last,
becomes a blessing in disguise.

When Jesus came to the point of saying, *Never-
theless, Father, not as I will, but as thou wilt,*[2]
he had overcome the world, even the appearance
of death. When we cease trying to force Life to
do our bidding and start agreeing with the Perfect Power within, through meditation, It will
live through us and we will find ways to live a
creative life. It is in deep meditation that we

[2]Matthew 26:39

experience the oneness of Life which is complete
agreement.

Meditation for Non-Resistance

Let us relax and be very quiet. Think to yourself: *I am letting go and letting God. I am completely relaxed. I am in complete accord with
Life. There is no resistance in me. I am in harmony with all of life.*

Silence

Nothing disturbs me.
I am centered in peace.
I am at peace.

Silence

I do not resist evil.
I trust the Perfect Power within me.
I agree with Life.

Silence

I let the Perfect Power live through me.
I know the peace that passes all
understanding.
I and the Father are one.

Silence

Chapter XI

HEALING—A BY-PRODUCT OF MEDITATION

In her book, THE BRAIN REVOLUTION, Marilyn Ferguson tells this story:

> *An Indian parable tells of a high government official who fell out of favor with his king and was imprisoned in a tower. One moonlight night the prisoner saw his wife far below. She was smearing honey on the antennae of a beetle. After fastening a silken thread to its body, she pointed the insect upward toward the tower window.*
>
> *Tempted by the smell of honey, the beetle kept crawling up the wall. Finally the prisoner caught it, removed the silken thread, and set the insect free. Pulling on the thread he found that it grew heavier and heavier. Attached to it was a length of sewing cotton and to that a heavy string, which itself was attached to a strong rope by which he escaped.*

The German writer, Paul Dessauer, who related the tale in NATURAL MEDITATION, added:

The first thing meditation brings in its train is very small—as insignificant as a silken thread drawn slowly up a high black wall at night by a small weak creature. This is the beginning of meditation. By repeating it, by persevering in repeating it, the silken thread becomes a cotton, then a string, then a cord, and at last a strong rope, which finally is able to bear the full weight of a man. [1]

For thousands of years people have known that meditation was beneficial to the physical well-being of the individual but there was no scientific evidence to this effect. Now meditation has reached that point where it bears the weight of a man. Scientists are showing great interest in proving the effects of meditation on the physical body. In the past decade much has been revealed along these lines. The exciting thing that has come out of this scientific research is that we are now able to measure the changes in bodily activities brought about through meditation. This is done through what is called bio-feedback.

What Bio-Feedback Is

Thousands of years ago yogis were controlling the heart beat and the pulse rate through meditation. They found that they could even suspend

[1] Marilyn Ferguson, THE BRAIN REVOLUTION, (Taplinger Publishing Company, Inc., New York, 1973, Pg. 74).

the heart beat and live for periods of time in suspended animation. Today, through the use of scientific instruments, people are measuring the physical effects of mind control. Barbara B. Brown, Ph.D., in her excellent book, NEW MIND, NEW BODY, BIO-FEEDBACK: NEW DIRECTIONS FOR THE MIND, has this to say about bio-feedback:

> *Bio-feedback is the newest, most exciting and potentially farthest-reaching discovery ever to emerge from the busy basement of biomedical research. It has been a virtual explosion of discovery, and it is currently causing a revolution in both scientific and public thinking. Sometimes called Bio-Feed-back Training (BFT), the new phenomenon is a mind-machine communciations tech-nique which, for the first time, allows man to communicate with his inner self . . . .*

> *The discovery allows man to sense signals of his own internal body activities and then to translate these signals into outward signs that he can observe to learn what is going on inside of himself. The consequence of this rather ordinary business of sampling a per-son's internal activity, with methods much like those used in every medical examination, is the new magic of the mind. For once a person tunes himself (rather than the doctor tuning in) to monitors of his internal being, be they a moving index of body temperature*

or the complexities of his brain waves, that
person becomes acquainted with his internal
behavior. And just as with his externally
directed behavior, with practice he can learn
to control it.[2]

Many doctors today are interested in research
in bio-feedback. Out of this are coming many
interesting and exciting developments. It was our
privilege to attend a Seminar at the University of
California at Los Angeles where we heard Dr.
Barbara Brown, Dr. Elmer Green and Dr. Carl
Simonton speak.

Dr. Elmer Green of the Menninger Foundation
reports that he has obtained many records demon-
strating the ability of an Indian yogi subject to
stop his heart for considerable periods of time,
ten to thirty seconds.

Dr. Green's psychophysiological principle as he
stated it, is: *Every change in the physiological*
state is accompanied by an appropriate change
in the mental-emotional state, conscious or un-
conscious . . . and conversely, every change in
the mental-emotional state, conscious or uncon-
scious, is accompanied by an appropriate change
in the physiological state.

Where have we heard this before? William
James, often called the father of modern psy-
chology, said: *The greatest discovery of my life-*

[2]Barbara B. Brown, Ph.D., NEW MIND, NEW BODY,
BIO-FEEDBACK: NEW DIRECTIONS FOR THE MIND,
(Harper and Row, New York, NY 1974).

time was that a person can change the circumstances of his life by changing his thoughts and his attitudes. Now modern science has come up with a method of proving these interesting ideas through bio-feedback.

Dr. Elmer Green is intensely interested in creativity as it relates to thoughts that come in sleep and near sleep, and he believes that the stabilizing influence in bio-feedback research by the amateur is meditation.

Cancer Healed Through Meditation

To us who are so interested in meditation, the most exciting part of the entire Seminar was Dr. Carl Simonton's contribution.

Dr. Carl Simonton, a recognized cancer and meditation researcher, was former chief of radiological therapy at Travis Air Force Base near Sacramento, California. His credentials in the medical profession in radiology are tops, having graduated from the University of Oregon Medical School and taken graduate work there in radiology. He was not happy with this work because he did not feel that the methods used were getting any positive results. He began searching to find what it was that happened in the very small number of people who did recover. He said that he began to try to find what the people who had recovered were thinking about. This entailed considerable research because he had to find colleagues and records that could be helpful along these lines. He began looking at winners and seeing what they had in common. He found that the commonality was in the attitude. In the first place, they wanted to get well and in the second place, they had a very interesting attitude toward life. The spontaneous-remission patients were optimistic, positive individuals. If positive attitudes made all the difference, the next great question he asked himself was, *How do you teach attitudes?*

He took a little detour here and went outside the medical field to study sales philosophy, attitude controls, mind control, bio-feedback devices for measuring controls, alpha waves and alpha feedback. He began to see how attitudes could be changed. He realized that you cannot change the situation *unless you can change the thinking of a person.*

On Sunday, April 4, 1971, he came to the conclusion that this was the path that he would take, the path of primarily applying a change of attitude together with any necessary accepted therapy from the medical point of view. He told of how he applied this aproach to his first patient the next day. He said that had he had to wait for any period of time to put his new idea to work he might not have tried it. He was very much afraid of this. It was fortunate that right when he got the idea he was able to apply it to the very first patient. His technique has basically not changed since that time.

This first case was so dramatic that it definitely

proved to him that he was on the right track and that he should continue to pursue it. The patient was a sixty-one year old gentleman with a far advanced throat cancer. As he talked with him he found that the patient's weight had gone from 135 pounds down to 95 pounds. He could not eat. In fact, he could barely swallow his own saliva and had great difficulty breathing. He was very weak. Dr. Simonton said, *He was a tremendous little man.*

Dr. Simonton explained to him the principles he had in mind and some of the thinking behind what he intended to do. The patient was to sit in a comfortable position and slowly breathe in and out and every time he breathed out he was to mentally say to himself the word, *relax.* He was to concentrate on relaxing the muscles around his eyes and around his jaws and he was to do this for no more than a minute and a half to two minutes at a time. Then in this relaxed state he would visualize a pleasant scene, something from his past which made him feel pleasurable. This for no more than a minute or a minute and a half and then he was to picture his tumor as the doctor had explained it to him. Then he was to picture the radiation therapy, the way the bullets of energy intereact with both the normal and the tumor cells, that the normal cells were much more active than the cancer cells and would repair themselves and the tumor cells would die. Then he was to meditate on his own immunity mechanism, the white blood cells coming in and picking up the dead or dying cancer cells and picture the body doing the repair work.

He was told to do this three times a day, the first thing when he got up in the morning, right after lunch, and at night, the last thing before he got into bed.

Dr. Simonton marvelled that such was the man's determination that during seven weeks of treatment he failed to do this only one time and that was when someone interfered with his day and he got upset with that individual. He had an unexpectedly good response. In the beginning, he had been given a five to ten percent curability, but he got over his cancer by using this meditation treatment which Dr. Simonton worked out for him.

About that time, Dr. Simonton was drafted and was assigned to Travis Air Force Base. Dr. Simonton reported that this patient came to Travis after his throat was well and told him how he had applied the same principle to arthritis. After his arthritis was gone he was able to go back fishing. And then he called the doctor a couple of weeks later and told him how he had applied the same principle to impotence. The man had been impotent for twenty years. At that time he was in his early forties. It took him ten days of picturing the problem and the solution before he was able to successfully have intercourse with his wife. The cure was lasting.

Dr. Simonton told us, *By this time, you could*

hardly keep me from bouncing off the walls! It was this first successful adventure into meditation that gave him the courage to go ahead and use these techniques with his patients.

Not only did Dr. Simonton tell us about his successful treatment of cancer patients but he showed us slides taken week by week showing the progress of the healing. This, he said, was for the purpose of educating the viewer just as he educates every cancer patient who comes to him. The slides actually did show the cancer disappearing until there was no remnant left.

The two premises upon which he bases his technique are:

1. The normal state of the body is a healthy state.
2. Everybody has had cancer, at some time or another.

He said that most people do not realize that all of us probably have had cancer about several thousand times during our lifetimes. And that our bodies recognize these cells as abnormal and destroy them. We never know that we had it. It is much like tuberculosis, the common cold and other things that are ubiquitous in our society. When we realize this, cancer suddenly loses its strong emotionalism. We can then look at it as a regular disease.

When he had finished, we, too, were literally "bouncing off the walls." We had known of cancer healings, even instantaneous healings, but here was a medical doctor using meditation with spectacular results. Spiritual healings are always hard to document. Here were healings through a form of meditation, that were clearly documented.

Meditation

I turn my attention away from any thought of sickness.
My life is one with the Life of God and that Life is perfect.

Silence

Now picture some beautiful, restful scene that you remember—a brilliant sunrise, a quiet lake with the mist rising slowly from it—whatever brings you a feeling of peace.

Silence

Now think of your body as glowing with Light. It is, you know. Every cell, every atom is Light.

Silence

Think of the perfect Life of God in every muscle, every bone, every tissue, every cell, every atom.

Silence

Claim for yourself: *I am pure Spirit. I am God Life.*

Silence

Chapter XII

COSMIC CONSCIOUSNESS, THE ULTIMATE JOY

We have considered the benefits of meditating and the joy of meditation. Now we come to the ultimate joy, that blissful state known as Cosmic Consciousness. The Indian yogi calls it *Nirvana*. The Christian mystic may call it *experiencing God*. This illumination that comes to a few, in varying degrees, is always a realization of oneness with the Universal One. Even a glimpse of this glorious state is enough to change a person forever. Those who have achieved it draw others to them as a magnet draws steel filings. They seek the illumined one, yet do not realize what draws them.

Meditation—The Royal Road

Meditation is the royal road to this ultimate experience that transcends all others. *Bliss* is a word often associated with the cosmic experience. The dictionary definition of bliss is *serene happiness*. Cosmic Consciousness is serene happiness.

Unlike transient, earthly joys it leaves an indelible impression. Once known, the soul hungers for it again. All else pales by comparison.

Medical Doctor Experiences Cosmic Consciousness

At the beginning of the 20th century, a medical doctor named Richard Bucke wrote a book entitled COSMIC CONSCIOUSNESS, A STUDY IN THE EVOLUTION OF THE HUMAN MIND. In this book, he prophesied not only a social revolution in this century, but a psychical revolution as well. In it he describes and documents what he calls Cosmic Consciousness, *a consciousness of the cosmos, that is, of the life and order of the universe.*[1]

In describing his own experience, Dr. Bucke proclaimed that along with the consciousness of the cosmos, there occurs an intellectual enlightenment or illumination which alone would place the individual on a new plane of existence — would make him almost a member of a new species. To this is added a state of moral exaltation, an indescribable feeling of elevation, elation, and joyousness, and a quickening of the moral sense which is fully as striking and of more importance to the individual and to the race than is the enhanced intellectual power. With this comes

[1]Richard Bucke, COSMIC CONSCIOUSNESS, (New York: E.P. Dutton and Company, Inc.). (First edition by Innes & Sons, 1901).

what may be called a sense of immortality, a consciousness of eternal life.

Bucke believed that within this century our descendents would sooner or later, as a race, achieve Cosmic Consciousness. He believed that this step in psychic evolution was, even in his time, in the process of being made. It is interesting to note that his treatise on Cosmic Consciousness has had a revival in popularity and is being widely read today, especially by young people. Bucke believed that the psychic evolution going on in this century would literally create a new heaven and a new earth; that all would be made new.

Suppose for the moment that we agree with him, believing his prophecy to be true. What is the best possible way to bring it about? It is not surprising that, in this drug oriented society of today, it seemed natural to some that popping a pill into the mouth, or smoking a drug, or injecting a drug into the veins, might be the answer to our glorious destiny. This proved to be a snare and a delusion.

The Way to Cosmic Consciousness

The open door to Cosmic Consciousness is, of course, meditation. Historically those who have been caught up into exalted states of spiritual consciousness have spent hours in meditation.

There was Gautama the Buddha as he sat under the Bo tree; Jesus the Christ, *I and the*

Father are one; Paul on the road to Damascus; Plotinus; Mohammed; Dante; Francis Bacon; William Blake; Walt Whitman — to name a few. Having had the experience of Cosmic Consciousness they became a special breed to whom others were drawn not always knowing why they came, but impelled by an irresistable urge to partake of what they sensed the uplifted ones had. Many were drawn to read the works of Walt Whitman but not all were ready to receive the message. The same is true of Jesus and the others. We sense that there is a treasure to be had from their words but we are not always ready to accept it. As someone once said, we have to be able to write the Bible ourselves before we can completely understand it — we have to have had a measure of spiritual experience to understand what the prophets were trying to tell us.

The Many Names that Have Been Given to Cosmic Consciousness

Because Jesus, the Christ, so beautifully exemplified the Cosmic Consciousness, it is called Christ Consciousness. The word *Christ* comes from the Greek, *Khristos,* meaning *the anointed one.* Jesus, himself, did not adopt the title. It was given him by his followers who understood the Christ Consciousness. Jesus called the exalted state: the Kingdom of *Heaven* and *the Kingdom of God* (within you). Paul called it Christ — *Christ*

*in you, the hope of glory . . . I live, yet not I,
Christ liveth in me.* He spoke of being *in Christ,*
of having *that mind which was also in Christ Jesus.*

Let's see what others have called it. Bucke
likened it to *a duplex personality* shared by those
who had experienced Cosmic Consciousness.
*Mohammed called the cosmic sense "Gabriel,"
and seems to have looked upon it as a distinctly
separate person who lived in him and spoke to
him. Dante called it "Beatrice" ("Making Happy"),
a name almost or quite equivalent to "Kingdom
of Heaven." Balzac called the new man a "spe-
cialist" and the new condition "specialism." Whitman called cosmic consciousness "My Soul," but
spoke of it as if it were another person . . .* [2]

It would seem that Jesus and the apostles knew
more about the experience of Cosmic Consciousness than we might imagine. Paul admonished
the Ephesians and the Colosians to *put on the
new man.* He said that he was caught up into
the third heaven, paradise. Paradise means *a
state of heavenly bliss.* In the day of Pentecost
they were all filled with the Holy Spirit. [3]

Not Reserved for a Few

The tendency, in looking backward in history,
is to feel excluded from such glorious adventures
as something which was forever reserved for a few

[2] Bucke, *op. cit.,* p. 62
[3] Acts 2:4, RSV

great ones, never to be dreamed possible for ourselves. And, if we do have a glimpse of Cosmic Consciousness we are so awed by the experience that we feel shy about revealing it to others; for who would believe such a thing about us?

Finally, having made bold to tell our story we find others encouraged to share also.

I quote a recent letter:

I read your story about experiencing the white light. I, too, had a similar experience in a little different way. Over eight years ago I was a problem drinker. I went on a week's binge and became scared. I didn't know where to turn so I called A.A. A young man came to see me and asked me to pray with him. At this point in my life I had forgotten about God. I was an agnostic.

As we prayed together, I felt a pain beyond description. As the hours dragged on, my friend had fallen asleep. In front of me appeared a brilliant golden light that seemed to be in one area, yet it filled the room. I was filled with peace and love and I realized that all my pain had vanished. I, too, was reluctant to tell anyone about my experience. Later on, I felt that there was a reason why I had the experience and part of the reason was that I might share it with other people who were also searching for answers. I prayed to God for His help and this was my answer.

It Changes One Completely

His name was Saul before his great spiritual experience on the road to Damascus. The light that shined about him changed his nature so completely that thereafter he was known as Paul. Paul seems to have a sense of deep humility in discussing his cosmic experience. He spoke of it in his second letter to the Corinthians,

> *It is not expedient for me doubtless to glory, I will come to visions and revelations of the Lord.*
>
> *I knew a man in Christ above fourteen years ago, (whether in the body, I cannot tell; or whether out of the body, I cannot tell: God knoweth;) such an one caught up to the third heaven. And I knew such a man, (whether in the body, or out of the body, I cannot tell: God knoweth:)*
>
> *How that he was caught up into paradise, and heard unspeakable words, which it is not lawful for a man to utter.*
>
> *Of such an one will I glory: yet of myself I will not glory, but in mine infirmities.*
>
> *For though I would desire to glory, I shall not be a fool; for I will say the truth: but now I forbear, lest any man should think of me above that which he seeth me to be, or that he heareth of me.*[4]

The ancient Hebrews believed that there were

[4]II Corinthians 12:1

seven heavens inhabited by varying grades of superhumans, the highest, or aravoth, being reserved for God. It was Paradise, or the third heaven, to which Paul said he had been caught up.

Paul was referring to a personal experience in which he was exalted, lifted up in consciousness to such an extent that it seemed he was another person. When he says *I knew a man who was caught up to the third heaven,* he is referring to the spiritual Self that experienced Cosmic Consciousness. Each one who has had the experience, in looking back, is reluctant to claim it as an experience of the present man.

Don Blanding was so changed by his cosmic experience that he tore up a manuscript he had just finished. His writing was quite different from that time on. He described his spiritual experience to us personally and later told of it from the platform. Each time he became so emotional that it was hard for him to speak.

Don, a gregarious fellow by nature had, for some reason unknown to himself at the time, gone on a freighter trip. He found the captain was a loner who preferred to stay by himself and the crew didn't speak English. There was no one to talk to. He felt such aloneness as he had never known. Somewhere out in the blue Pacific, to use his own expression, he *died at dawn.* It was this moving experience that caused him to tear up one manuscript and write: JOY IS AN INSIDE JOB.

Afterward, in attempting to describe the experience, he said:

> *Nothing changed, yet everything changed . . . from Simple Consciousness to Self-Consciousness to Cosmic or Veritable Consciousness . . . "God saw everything that he had made, and behold . . . it was very good." I know the futility of trying to prove anything verbally. But I can testify happily that with the deep realization that in the Power of the Presence of God-Consciousness, not as a remote and distant thing to be plead for, but as an immediate and ever-present power, awaiting only recognition and acceptance, lies the Land of Joy-Age or the Kingdom of Heaven, or the Peace of Heart which is beyond any other treasure, tangible or intangible, in the world.* [5]

Being a poet, he expressed it poetically; but, we can testify that he was a changed man. Especially his writing which was now on a much higher plane than anything he had written before.

Cosmic Consciousness is Not Self-Induced

Cosmic Consciousness is not something that we will to happen. We all agree the mind-expanding

[5] Don Blanding, JOY IS AN INSIDE JOB, (New York: Dodd, Mead & Co., 1953).

experience is highly desirable. But, it must be accomplished in a natural way. You cannot storm the gates of heaven. You cannot make your mind expand without doing yourself harm. It is a letting process. Paul said: *Let this mind be in you that was also in Christ Jesus.* Let means to allow, to permit. I repeat in a paraphrase: *Permit, or allow this mind to be in you which was also in Christ Jesus.* The higher awareness is attained through letting. You are already a child of God. You are already a son of the Most High. You are already heir to the Kingdom. Through meditation you put aside your inhibitions, your false beliefs and fears and become ready to receive spiritually. Through meditation we bring our thoughts into alignment with the Divine. When we become still enough, the Universal Intelligence is able to commune with us. Meditation leads to the revelation of our oneness with Divine Consciousness which Emerson called the Over Soul. But, the actual experience of being caught up into Cosmic Consciousness usually comes when we least expect it. We are awakened out of sleep, or we may be doing some mundane thing when it comes.

An English Mystic Reveals His Cosmic Experience

I remember hearing Brother Mandus, an English mystic, relate his cosmic experience. He said it came about quite unexpectedly one evening while he was wiping the dishes for his wife. It came without warning, but not without hours of meditative preparation, in the days preceding. Ever after, he recalled it as the greatest experience of his life, an experience that changed him and changed his life. It revealed to him the gift of healing, and drew people to him from all over the world. In his book, THIS WONDROUS WAY OF LIFE, he speaks of his great experience:

> . . . *that vital moment when I was baptized by the Holy Spirit within. For one perfect second, unexpected, unheralded, and while I was doing a trivial task, my personal mind and body were fused in LIGHT: a breathless, unbearable LIGHT-PERFECTION as intense as the explosion of a flash of lightning within me . . . In this timeless second I knew a Love, Wisdom, Knowledge, and Ecstasy transcending anything I could understand or describe. I was lifted into the midst of God in whom all people, all worlds, and every created life or thing moved and had their being. Perfection! Had I been suffering from the worst mental or physical disease known to man, in that LIGHT I should instantly have been made WHOLE.* [6]

Brother Mandus said that he never again had this great experience. He said that it was not

[6] Brother Mandus, THIS WONDROUS WAY OF LIFE, (London, L.N. Fowler & Co. Ltd., 1956).

necessary. Forever afterward he was able to sustain it in the midst of every other experience. As he said, he was never again the same.

A Very Personal Story

Cornelia knows how Paul felt, for in telling of her cosmic experience she is inclined to say *"I knew a woman who . . ."* It was during a period of great stress during which she had spent considerable time in prayer and meditation. Finally she reached the point where she could not pray any more. The problem seemed so insurmountable that she surrendered her life completely to the Almighty Power. *Here I am, Father, take me over. Do what you will with me!* After that she experienced a great sense of peace, having abandoned herself completely to God. It didn't matter what happened after that. For the first time in weeks she slept. Some time during the night she was awakened by a Voice that seemed to come from many echo chambers. The Voice said: *DON'T YOU TRUST ME?* All around her there was a warm, bright LIGHT. She felt as if she had been lifted up above the bed as on a down comforter into this beautiful, all-absorbing LIGHT. "Yes, yes," she answered, "I do!" Then there was an awareness of oneness with all of Life, oneness with all people, all creation, every part of Life. It was a moment of complete fulfillment, indescribable bliss, a never-to-be-forgotten experience. She described it as a melting sensation, a time of melting into Life. Something happened to her that changed her forever. She would never again be the same person. For more than a year after that she retained the *melting sensation*. No matter what happened she was able to recapture the moment of Oneness so that she could at will eliminate all tension and relive the melting feeling with all of Life.

Her Whole Being was Flooded With a Great Light

Nona Brooks who later became co-founder of the Divine Science Church in Denver, Colorado, was at one time in very poor physical condition, being able to eat only very soft, specially prepared food. For more than a year, according to her own account, she had been praying almost constantly, "God, give me light." A woman in her church started informal classes to tell of a miraculous healing that she had received. In DIVINE SCIENCE, ITS PRINCIPLE AND PRACTICE, Nona Brooks tells of her experience in the Light.

It was during the fourth class lesson, which eight of us were taking with Mrs. Bingham, that my whole being was completely flooded with a great light—a light brighter than sunlight, brighter than any I had ever seen. It filled me! It surrounded me! I was conscious of nothing but that intense light! I thought that of course all in the room had seen the light too, but they had not. I alone had had this wonderful experience. I discovered that I had been instantly and completely healed. Though the actual healing was instantaneous, yet I truly believe that the months and months of praying that I might receive light had been a preparation for the healing which had actually come to me in the form of light. [7]

Richard Bucke Tells His Own Cosmic Experience

Bucke, himself, tells his experience as if he were talking about another person:

It was in the early spring, at the beginning of his thirty-sixth year. He and two friends had spent the evening reading Wordsworth, Shelley, Keats and Browning, and especially Whitman. They parted at midnight, and he had a long drive in a hansom (it was in an English city). His mind, deeply under the influence of the ideas, images and emotions called up by the reading and talk of the evening, was calm and peaceful. He was in a state of quiet, almost passive enjoyment. All at once, without warning of any kind, he

[7]Nona Lovell Brooks, DIVINE SCIENCE, Its Principle and Practice (Denver, Colorado: Divine Science Church and College, 1957).

found himself wrapped around as it were by a flame-colored cloud. For an instant he thought of fire, some sudden conflagration in the great city; the next, he knew that the light was within himself. Directly afterwards came upon him a sense of exultation, of immense joyousness accompanied or immediately followed by an intellectual illumination quite impossible to describe. Into his brain streamed one momentary lightning-flash of Brahmic Splendor which has ever since lightened his life; upon his heart fell one drop of Brahmic Bliss, leaving thenceforward for always an aftertaste of heaven. Among other things he did not come to believe, he saw and knew that the Cosmos is not dead matter but a living Presence, that the soul of man is immortal, that the universe is so built and ordered that without any peradventure all things work together for the good of each and all, that the foundation principle of the world is what we call love and that the happiness of every one is in the long run absolutely certain. [8]

Still speaking in the third person, Bucke claims that he learned more within those few seconds than in previous months and even years of study; that the illumination itself continued not more than a few moments, but it was impossible for him ever to forget what, at that time, he saw and

[8]Bucke, *op. cit.*, p. 9

knew. He began to be very interested in the state of Cosmic Consciousness and, sought out others whom he considered to have spiritual insight and found that they, too, had entered this higher life.

Following his own introduction to Cosmic Consciousness, "The Doctor," as he was affectionately called, spent twenty-five years researching the matter of Illumination and Cosmic Consciousness. He wrote up more than fifty cases of Cosmic Consciousness and found that they all followed a similar pattern. He called this the *marks of the Cosmic Sense.* They all included:

1. The subjective light.
2. The moral elevation.
3. The intellectual illumination.
4. The sense of immortality.
5. The loss of fear of death.
6. The suddenness of the awakening.
7. The charm or magnetism added to the personality so that others are always thereafter drawn to the person.

He said that there were various degrees of illumination and the mere fact that a person had experienced it did not therefore make him omniscient or infallible, that there was still plenty of room for spiritual growth.

Cosmic Consciousness Not Exclusive Right of Men

Bucke seemed to think that Cosmic Consciousness was more apt to happen to men than to women; yet, two of his most beautiful accounts were told to him by women. The account that he considered the most outstanding example of all was given to him, also, by a woman who forbade him to use it in any way, not even anonymously.

Here is the case of a young woman who told her story to Richard Bucke. He identifies her only as C.Y.E. As with most of the men whose stories he recounts, she was in her thirties. Two years after her marriage, her husband became an enthusiastic and ardent admirer of the writings of Walt Whitman and there, to her great sorrow, she was left behind. She simply could not understand a word of "Leaves of Grass." It was as if it was written in an unknown tongue. Her husband found new men friends who shared his enthusiasm for Whitman but she became still more mystified. Then, one day, after she and her husband had been having long talks about Whitman and his teachings she had this unusual experience which she recounted to Bucke as follows:

> On the afternoon of Wednesday I went to see a friend, a farmer's wife, and we drove over the harvest fields to take some refreshment to her husband who was working with his men. When I was going away she gave me two very beautiful roses. I had always had a passionate love of flowers, but the scent of these and their exquisite form and color appealed to me with quite exceptional force and vividness. I left my friend and was

walking slowly homeward, enjoying the calm beauty of the evening, when I became conscious of an unutterable stillness, and simultaneously every object about me became bathed in a soft light, clearer and more ethereal than I had ever before seen. Then a voice whispered in my soul: "God is all. He is not far away in the heaven; He is here. This grass under your feet is He; this bountiful harvest, that blue sky, those roses in your hand—you yourself are all one with Him. All is well for ever and ever, for there is no place or time where God is not." Then the earth and air and sky thrilled and vibrated to one song, and the burden of it was "Glory to God in the highest and on earth, peace, good will toward men."

On my return home both my husband and his sister remarked a change in my face. An infinite peace and joy filled my heart, worldly ambitions and cares died in the light of the glorious truth that was revealed to me—all anxiety and trouble about the future had utterly left me, and my life is one long song of love and peace. When I awake in the night or rise from my bed in the morning—nay, at all hours of the day and night—the song is ever with me, "Glory to God in the highest, on earth, peace, good will toward men."[9]

As with the others whom Bucke interviewed,

[9]Bucke, *op. cit.*, p. 357

she gained a strong sense of immortality and
ceased to fret and worry over the problem of evil.
As for intellectual illumination, now she could
read Whitman, her soul eagerly drinking in his
words.

Illumination Makes Us One

Those who have shared great moments of
illumination know the bliss that cannot be con-
veyed to another for there are no words to explain
it except in figurative language—the ladder to
heaven with angels ascending and descending,
the dream that forever changed Jacob into Israel,
the prince of God; the heavenly host heard by the
Shepherds in the field *praising God and saying,
Glory to God in the highest, and on earth, peace,
good will toward men;* Paul's great light on the
road to Damascus; the New Jerusalem that appeared as a vision to John on the isle of Patmos;
the transfiguration of Jesus before two of his dis-
ciples on the mount—all were attempts by people
to explain the phenomenon of Cosmic Consciousness.

> *Does it matter that Paul and the poet
> Blake called the place of attainment the City
> of God, while the Buddha named it the City
> of Peace? that the Christians termed it the
> heavenly Jerusalem, while the Buddha spoke
> of it as the Universe of Delight?*
> *The blessed Buddha was one in an un-
> ending line of seers who have cried down the*

sense-ridden, self-infected mortal existence;
who have celebrated as the highest and holiest
aim of life the attainment of divine conscious-
ness or Enlightenment or spiritual rapture.
The "way" is by the fires of purgation, and
the end is immersion or absorption—in Nir-
vana, or in God. [10]

Poets, more than any other group, seem able
to express it. To quote that great mystic, William
Blake:

To see a World in a Grain of Sand
And a Heaven in a Wild Flower,
Hold Infinity in the palm of your hand,
And Eternity in an hour—

Meditation

I will listen for the Voice of God:

Silence

Thou art God, in Whom I have put my trust.
Thy Presence is everywhere.

Thy Presence surrounds me; in Thee I live and
move and have my being.

Thy Presence is within me, strengthening,
inspiring, healing and perfecting me.

[10]Sheldon Cheney, MEN WHO HAVE WALKED WITH
GOD, (New York: Alfred A. Knopf, 1948).

Thy Presence banishes fear and worry and anxiety.

Thy Presence gives me strength for all my needs.

Thy Presence gives me confidence and courage in every situation.

Thy Presence drives out resentment and hatred and subdues anger.

The inspiration of Thy Presence gives me understanding, that I may have clearness of vision, steadfastness of thought and trueness of speech.

Thy Presence enables me to overcome evil and disease in all forms.

Nothing can separate me from Thy Presence.

Silence

OUT OF THE SILENCE

There is a sense of urgency in the air.
There is a feeling that God wants to express
    Himself through me,
To live through me; but I do not feel worthy.
I do not feel good enough to be an instrument
    of God's perfect Life.
How can His wonders express through me?
How can His miracles be done through me?
Who am I that I should even think for a moment
    that this is possible?

Wait . . . What is that which You are saying so
    softly . . .
So quietly . . . and yet, so distinctly? Say it
    again . . .
    And in some other way, that I may be sure.
You . . . deep within the recesses of my soul . . .
    are You
Speaking the Truth or only leading me on? You
    whom I hear
Only in my quiet moments . . . my rare, quiet
    moments . . .
Are trying to tell me that you are the voice of
    God . . .
        The still, small voice.

But a Voice that resounds throughout my
    consciousness

With the roar of thunder. You are God, you say,
    and then, and then,
You say, You are Me!
        What? YOU are me?
Yes! I heard you . . . but can I believe You?
Hearing You is one thing . . . but believing You
    is another.
        This takes a lot of believing.

Did you say that I should prove You . . . by
    testing You . . .
By trying You . . . by being You . . . Well,
    all right, here goes!

I am being still and knowing that the "I AM"
    within me is God.
I am letting go of all feeling of directing and
    manipulating life.
I am letting Thy will be done through me.
        Of myself I do nothing.
It is You within me Who does the good works.
I am the Way, the Truth, and the Life.
    I am the Light that lighteth the heart of
    every man.
        I am THAT I am.

Not only do I hear your message, but I am now
    beginning to see your Truth.
It is *within* that the Kingdom is gained and won.
It is *within* that I find your Peace that passes
    all understanding.

It is within that the wonders and the glory of
    your perfect Love
Are found . . . not withdrawn from the world
    . . . but at the very
Center of Life. I thank Thee Father for revealing
    Thyself,
    Even a glimpse of Thyself to me.

Jack Ensign Addington

Also by Jack Ensign Addington

ALL ABOUT GOALS AND HOW TO ACHIEVE
   THEM
THE SECRET OF HEALING
PSYCHOGENESIS: Everything Begins in Mind
THE HIDDEN MYSTERY OF THE BIBLE
THE TRUTH ABOUT EMOTIONAL MATURITY
THE TRUTH ABOUT GOD
YOUR MIRACLE BOOK
PRAYER LEDGER
THE WAY OF HAPPINESS
HOW TO BUILD CONFIDENCE IN YOURSELF
LIFE NEVER DIES

With Cornelia Addington

YOUR NEEDS MET
I AM THE WAY
THE PERFECT POWER WITHIN YOU
THE JOY OF MEDITATION
ALL ABOUT PROSPERITY AND HOW YOU
   CAN PROSPER
DRAWING THE LARGER CIRCLE
THE WONDER-WORKING POWER OF GOD

Books may be ordered from Abundant Living Foundation, Box
100, San Diego, CA 92138. Current price list available upon re-
quest. Those interested in receiving Abundant Living magazine
are invited to write.

Distributed to the book trade by DeVorss & Company, Box
550, Marina del Rey, CA 90294.

ABOUT THE AUTHORS

For more than 30 years the Addingtons have worked closely together in the fields of writing and lecturing. Through its monthly publication the Abundant Living magazine, Abundant Living Foundation brings their teaching to thousands of people throughout the world.

Jack Addington attended the University of Florida at Gainesville, and has had three successful careers, first in business where he was a practicing attorney, then 20 years in the ministry, founding two large churches. In 1968 he retired from church work to begin his worldwide ministry. He now devotes his time to writing, lecturing, a large radio and prayer ministry, and his work in the prisons.

Cornelia Addington attended the University of Washington in Seattle where she majored in painting and design. She was successful as a designer for a large manufacturing firm, later going into interior design. During the past 30 years she has edited Dr. Addington's manuscripts and co-authored several of his books. She is the editor of the Abundant Living magazine and has had numerous articles published in national magazines.